Christy's Journey

Through Twelve Past Lives

Books by Peter Watson Jenkins:

Escape to Danger (*Watson Jenkins*)
1st Books Library (2001)

Training for The Marathon of Life
Resource Publications (2005)

Healing with the Universe, Meditation, and Prayer
Celestial Voices, Inc. (2007)

Talking with Leaders of the Past
Celestial Voices, Inc. (2008)

Christy's Journey
Through Twelve Past Lives

Peter Watson Jenkins

BOOKS

Winchester, U.K.
New York, U.S.A.

First published by O Books, 2008
O Books is an imprint of John Hunt Publishing
Ltd., The Bothy, Deershot Lodge, Park Lane,
Ropley, Hants, SO24 0BE, UK
office1@o-books.net
www.o-books.net

Distribution in:

UK and Europe
Orca Book Services
orders@orcabookservices.co.uk
Tel: 01202 665432 Fax: 01202 666219
Int. code (44)

USA and Canada
NBN
custserv@nbnbooks.com
Tel: 1 800 462 6420 Fax: 1 800 338 4550

Australia and New Zealand
Brumby Books
sales@brumbybooks.com.au
Tel: 61 3 9761 5535 Fax: 61 3 9761 7095

Far East (offices in Singapore, Thailand, Hong
Kong, Taiwan)
Pansing Distribution Pte Ltd
kemal@pansing.com
Tel: 65 6319 9939 Fax: 65 6462 5761

South Africa
Alternative Books
altbook@peterhyde.co.za
Tel: 021 555 4027 Fax: 021 447 1430

Text copyright Peter Watson Jenkins 2008

Design: Jim Weaver

ISBN: 978 1 84694 082 8

A CIP catalogue record for this book is available
from the British Library.

Printed in the US by Maple Vail

O Books operates a distinctive and ethical publishing philosophy in
all areas of its business, from its global network of authors to
production and worldwide distribution.

No trees were cut down to print this particular book. The paper is
100% recycled, with 50% of that being post-consumer. It's processed
chlorine-free, and has no fibre from ancient or endangered forests.
This production method on this print run saved approx. 13 trees,
4,000 gallons of water, 600 pounds of solid waste, 990 pounds of
greenhouse gases and 8 million Btu of energy. On its publication a
tree was planted in a new forest that O Books is sponsoring at The
Village www.thefourgates.com

Acknowledgements

My grateful thanks are due to:

"Christy" for her willing and lively involvement in this project.

My wife, Sonia A. Ness, for advising on the content and layout and for editing the manuscript.

Gail Gillispie for advice on ancient musical instruments.

John Hunt and his staff at O Books for publishing the book.

Contents

Introduction

You only live once, right?

Christy's gripping account of twelve previous earthly lives suggests otherwise. Her story is a compelling mixture of happiness and sadness, outright success and heartrending tragedy. She convincingly details her experiences of both genders and several ethnicities in various geographical and historical settings.

Christy is among the millions of people who have experienced past-life regression recently. You may even be one because the pace of regression work undertaken by psychiatrists, psychologists, and hypnotists has accelerated greatly during the past sixty years. It is estimated that more than five million individuals, in countries all over the world, have now been helped to look back on forgotten or half-remembered incidents in their past, either in conjunction with therapy or just to satisfy their curiosity. Some were deliberately guided into their past by their therapist; others went spontaneously. While it is easy to accept that hypnotism can help unlock the memories of childhood, many people are astonished to learn that the impressions of the unborn child can be readily recalled in hypnosis. For some folk, belief can be strained to the breaking point by the idea that rational individuals can settle down on a couch in the office of their therapist and in hypnotic trance take their memory back to life in their mother's womb – a time before they were even born. Nevertheless it happens frequently, and amazed parents have corroborated their adult children's accounts of events that neither had guessed the little baby could ever know. Regression experiences can be repeated precisely, each repetition of the event yielding more and more details as the memory of the hypnotized person clarifies. Nor does the wonder stop there. Often with considerable detail, hypnotized subjects have reported incidents from previous lives which they have experienced in trance. Regression into past lives takes people back in time not only to their immediate past life but sometimes to a whole series of lives, spanning hundreds of years and lived in different families and races, countries and continents. Their past life may have been lived as a man or as a woman. In fact it is somewhat rare for an individual subject only to appear in the same sex during a long series of incarnations.

Most people recall most of their past lives as poverty-stricken, uneventful, even boring. They were often brief lives by today's standards of longevity, frequently cut short by the early onset of disease, natural disaster, or violent acts. Reported past lives are very, very, very rarely anything that even modestly approaches the derided "I was Cleopatra" story you may have read about in supermarket fiction. Psychologist Dr. Helen Wambach has calculated that about seventy-five percent of recalled past lives were lived as poor people, twenty percent as middle-class business people, and no more than five percent as people of power or affluence. Few hypnotists have ever had a subject honestly report having lived the life of a famous historical person.

A feeling of wonder, even disbelief, at experiencing a past life may not be the only emotion people have following a regression. While many subjects delight at what they sense is a personal and remarkably spiritual breakthrough, others may see it as an intrusion into their existing belief system. It is often surprisingly difficult for the majority of subjects to identify *exactly* what their religious faith says about the phenomenon of past-life regression. Some others, who have learned second-hand about this kind of experience, react as if clinical hypnotists have played a dirty trick on their subjects through subtle suggestions, and so skeptics have created the myth that past-life regression is unwise at best and morally dangerous at worst. There are plenty of people who disbelieve past-life regression when they have never even tried it!

The religious issue does not stop with people's experience of past lives. Quite often accounts given by subjects include the report of their having a very positive continuing existence between their earthly lives. During these cosmic intervals of the "inter-life," the subjects recount that their spirits had a mixture of experiences. As we will see in the book, these include aimlessly wandering about upon the earth for a while after death, being stuck for a period in a dark and cold void, and (most frequently) traveling to a warm, bright, and welcoming realm which they describe as "The Other Side," or "The Light," or "Heaven," or, as most simply prefer, "Home."

Like my client Christy, you may be facing these issues for the very first time, or perhaps you have already read books by other therapists telling a similar story. Before Christy and I started the series of hypnosis sessions leading to the creation of this book, she told me that she had had no prior experience of hypnotism (except for the first regression session with me, which we did not record). She had never read a book about past lives or about psychic awareness. Bravely and generously, I thought, she agreed to become the subject of a lengthy and detailed enquiry about her own distant past, not just for the sake of the experience itself but also for the enlightenment of people with whom our report might eventually be shared.

Undergoing past-life regression can be rather daunting. You just don't know what you're getting yourself into when you begin. It may feel a bit impersonal at times, rather like viewing a recording of someone on television, but usually it is far too emotionally draining to be dismissed as a mere hallucination, and far too earthy simply to be called a spiritual vision. You discover that what is being revealed is the ongoing record of your personal life as a spirit.

Oliver Cromwell once instructed his portrait painter to picture him "warts and all." In our experience of past lives we find ourselves depicted honestly, the bad stuff about us thoroughly mixed in with the good. This was exactly the kind of experience that Christy had in her twelve past lives, recounted here.

In a Christmas poem, the British poet laureate John Betjeman asked insistently about Christ's nativity, "And is it true? And is it true?" Hypnotists often hear the same demand for verification of stories told concerning past lives. Some therapists actually fear the possibility of spoiling their professional reputation by admitting that past-life regression may be true which has led them to remain cautiously neutral, saying, "It's the client's experience, not mine." They suggest that their subjects may be randomly drawing from a cosmic storehouse of human memory, and talk knowingly about psychologist Carl Jung's theory concerning humanity's *Collective Unconscious*, as if his hypothesis were absolutely settled for all time as the whole truth. Other therapists see past-life accounts as a jumble of hallucinations, together with some drawing from a collective human memory, and maybe also some genuine individual recall.

According to surveys, the overwhelming majority of professional past-life regressionists do feel positively certain that most (but not all) of the past-life, and inter-life experiences recounted by their subjects really do ring true. However, all good therapists readily admit that, as their subject's subconscious mind seeks to come up with an answer to satisfy the therapist's latest question, sometimes the experience is just a simple hallucination. So when it comes to interpreting past-life regression, as fairground stall-keepers in London used to say in the days of Queen Victoria, "*Yer pays yer money, and yer takes yer choice!*"

We can believe in past lives as real or less than real, as the fancy suits us. But as the number of such experiences grows and grows, those who wish to tell us that the whole idea is hogwash discover that they must work ever harder to maintain their skeptical point of view. Huge numbers of therapists and their subjects have been hard at work on past-life regressions for over half a century now. A few years ago Jeffrey Ryan, President of the International Association of Regression Research and Therapies, claimed that specialist practitioners who are also IARRT members are calculated to have conducted over 2,500,000 individual past-life regressions since 1980. There are also just as many non-members, all over the world doing the job, and their numbers are accelerating fast.

Academic studies have been written on this subject and a variety of issues seriously debated. Yet the world of science remains largely indifferent to this quantity of research, and people in established religions sometimes show real hostility to its cautious conclusions. Never mind some positive statements in biblical texts; never mind the Christian church's ancient practice of exorcism, and all the talk by the religious – from Roman Catholics, to Fundamentalist Christians, to Muslims and to Jews – about angels and eternal life. Many people just don't like to face the uncertainty that the challenge of past-life regression poses to established scientific or theological positions. Regression implies that we take the idea of reincarnation seriously, and it threatens the neat theories of the physicists and the control freaks among the religious who tell you in all sincerity that "you've only got one life to get it right!"

As you will read, in answer to my questioning the hypnotized Christy tells her story very plainly. Her statements are spontaneous, somewhat laconic but straightforward, and her comments after our sessions are without pretense. This absorbing account of Christy's soul's journey makes no claim to be a unique example of past-life regression. On the contrary, it is recorded here in this book because it belongs fair and square to the realm of the everyday regression experience of practitioners like me. Christy's story could be your own, or one told by a family member or a friend. That's a very important point. Nowhere does Christy's intensely personal account make any scientific or religious claims – she has nothing to gain and no philosophy to peddle by telling her story.

The journey of her soul over twelve of its prior lives was remembered sometimes a little imperfectly but always to the best of her ability. Christy knows that she has further spiritual journeying still to do. So have we all.

First Meeting with Christy

When we first met in the fall of 2002, Christy was a 22-year-old who had recently graduated with high honors from a British university and was spending a year working in America as an intern in an arts organization. Her ready, genuine smile and ability to talk easily with wit and interest about a wide range of topics came with an unusually adventurous personality. Her cheerful laugh hid from us both the anguish and dark secrets she had locked inside her distant memory. Collecting the story of her soul's journey as it traveled from Ancient Rome to the present day was work which I did while on the staff of the Garrett Hypnosis Wellness Center in Chicago.

I am a clinical hypnotist and writer, having formerly worked as a minister of religion. I recruited Christy to record people's names and collect their fees at a "Stop-Smoking-with-Hypnosis" event at the Garrett Center one snowy day in January 2003. Despite my having spent a small fortune on advertising the event, however, nobody actually braved the snow and turned up. The two of us had nothing better to do so we chatted for half an hour, mostly about hypnotism.

Christy had a minor personal problem, which gave me the excuse to offer her a free hypnosis session to compensate for the waste of her time. She was a talented folk musician who had never mastered the skill of singing and playing from musical notation, although she had received several years of music training in high school. She said that she really wanted to deal with this mental block. In a sense Christy did not need to read musical notation because her ear was so sharp and her memory so good that she had only to hear a tune once or twice before being able to repeat it perfectly. It was an interesting problem to deal with, but if we failed to find the answer she would still be perfectly capable of performing.

She was a little ambivalent about her home background. Her happily married parents lived in the countryside of England. Her father had been a company executive for many years, while her mother worked for the government. Despite their comfortable, single-family home, Christy perceived that the family was not truly affluent, and she once asked her father if they were middle class or working class. Her question rang true as part of the uncertainty she felt about herself and her destiny – a feeling that might have had deeper roots than she knew.

In her initial hypnotic experience, Christy proved to be an excellent subject. Her clear recall and the ease with which she accessed subconscious memories sparked my idea of setting up a number of sessions in which we would trace her soul's path of discovery, eventually using the transcripts of our taped interviews to form the nucleus of a book.

When Christy generously consented to be my subject for this project, I recounted to her the unhappy experience of the late Virginia Morrow, who was the subject in Morey Bernstein's groundbreaking 1956 book about past-life regression, *The Search For Bridey Murphy*. Virginia lived to regret bitterly having being "discovered" and pestered by representatives of the media. In consequence "Christy" took the wise decision to conceal her true identity and has requested that her privacy be respected. I am unable, therefore, to thank Christy publicly by her real name for her patience and valuable contribution to our understanding of the nature of the soul's progression through successive lives. She richly deserves our thanks.

This is what Christy Wrote

To give you a feel for her present personality I asked her to jot down some notes about herself:

"Who am I? I like seeing myself as a friend to those close to me. My most rewarding role in life is being with my friends and helping them. My family is very important to me, and is wonderfully supportive. "There's a variety of things I'd like to accomplish. I aspire to be a professional musician. That's something I'm just going to have to shut-up-and-prove-if-it's-true. I believe it is true, but sometimes I don't act as if I want it to be. "I enjoy dancing, which I prefer to athletics. I was an actor at high school but not at university. Reading aloud is enjoyable. I used to make films as part of my college course but learning about the stuff seemed to kill the desire.

"I know that, if I finally learned to read music, I wouldn't have to stop learning things by ear, but it feels like that's what it would mean. I find learning by ear so rewarding, so much fun, and so exciting. It's almost more fun because I can't do it any other way. When I try to learn how to read music, once I put the book away, it's gone as if I had never read it. I don't know if I'm making myself do that to preserve the aural talent.

"Fulfilling my potential is my main worry, both musically and in other areas of my life. A lack of confidence is the big thing. It's contradictory because in some situations I'm without any doubt of my confidence and my ability to succeed. I know I've got plenty of great talents. I did so well at high school, there was an expectation that I was just going to breeze through. That is why going to university and not landing on my feet instantly was an eye opener.

"I feel it more keenly now, because I accomplished things musically at a young age, when I had no need for confidence. It did not occur to me that one day I would have doubts about these things. I had been playing piano since I was four. Later on, it occurred to me that I would be playing better were it not for my decision not to read music. I do want to play the piano. There have been times at the piano when I've been unable to play. That freaks me out! So the most important thing for me to achieve is to play piano, whatever form it takes."

Working with Hypnosis

As I mentioned, Christy was a very good hypnotic subject. From the outset she went rapidly into that state of relaxed-but-focused concentration which is hypnosis. As a clinical hypnotist looking back on the sessions, I have wondered whether her ease of going into hypnosis made me a little less interested in her depth of trance than I should have been. This is a debatable issue. Many psychiatrists just use a general relaxation technique on their patients to lead them into both present-life and past-life regression. No special emphasis has been placed by these practitioners on the depth of trance. On the other hand, experts may prefer to use a deep trance to achieve their objectives. There are problems both ways: with light trance some details of a life may be harder for a subject to recall, but with deep trance there is evidence of a greater transfer of the therapist's thoughts and mental images to the subject, who may hallucinate more in consequence.

I aimed at a moderately deep hypnosis, which professionals might describe as a *theta* level. As the mind is always moving up and down within the trance state this can only be a generalization. With this moderate level of trance we covered more ground at the expense of some detail that would have been achieved with greater depth. It was a choice that ultimately I do not regret making.

How the Story is Told

Although the book is largely laid out chronologically, with the exception of Hector's story, this was not the order in which we arrived at Christy's individual past lives. We started with Eleanor the Harpist but then examined the twentieth-century lives of Joyce and Peter because Christy had expressed a desire not to be mired in her distant past. Then we filled in the gap.

In order to aid us to be thorough and to discover all the past lives from Eleanor's birth in 1275 to Christy's own in 1980, she twice visited (in trance) the cosmic "Akashic library" where the celestial database of all our lives is held energetically. These visits were less helpful than we had hoped, because some pages of Christy's book of record simply refused to open at lives not previously explored by her. Blocking information is a fairly common occurrence with such regression; I just had not expected it to happen at the Akashic library. Christy seemed a little drained by the library experience, perhaps because her investigation had been partially blocked. Our final search of the past – the search that revealed Hector's life in Ancient Rome – was conducted mainly to find the cause of an outbreak of eczema around Christy's ear and on her elbows, but also out of curiosity at the possibility of discovering a much earlier life experience.

This book does not pretend to tell the whole story of Christy's many previous lives (which probably number in scores). However, we believe that the time we spent working in hypnosis and transcribing the recordings was more than sufficient to show the patterns of Christy's past, and the progression through the centuries of the issues with which she has recently been dealing. Between people's lives there are usually gaps of earth-time spent by the discarnate (out-of-the-body) spirit in adjustment, recovery, reflection, and preparation for the next incarnation.

Studies, such as those by Dr. Helen Wambach (*Reliving Past Lives* and *Life Before Life*), have suggested there may be a tendency for spirits to return to earth with greater frequency as human history has progressed. In fact the gaps between Christy's past lives were not especially large. It seems that her more fruitful and happy lives have generally been followed by a speedier turnaround at Home and more rapid re-entry into another human existence. That is reasonable because the process of the spirit ridding itself of severe earthly traumatic experiences clearly takes longer. There was one instance of Christy's spirit wandering the earth near to her old home for years after her death as Eleanor. On the other hand, the return Home was much more rapid after Sophie's deeply satisfying life.

Editorial Note

In the following passages, a small amount of editing of the recorded accounts of our lengthy hypnosis sessions has been thought desirable. This has slightly reduced the number of questions posed by the hypnotist by running together a few of Christy's briefest answers. Unsuccessful questioning (that received no reply) has been omitted. No substantial changes have been made either to the questions or the responses, or about information regarding dates, places, and names provided by Christy, though I have chosen to record in the text either her initial response or her later clarification. I encouraged Christy to write notes on her lives as she thought fit. These drew from her experience but none of them was written immediately afterwards, so they are more distant and fully conscious reflections on what her subconscious felt and saw in its memory recall. However, short-term memories of lives recalled by subjects from the distant past can remain in sharp focus for several weeks. They stay with us, often with much greater detail then reported initially, but they do become increasingly subject to interpretation by our conscious mind. For a young lady like Christy, who has a strong interest in the works of J. R. R. Tolkein, some unintended Middle Earth interpretation of material after the event is a real possibility, so her notes are quite separate from the question-and-answer session.

1

Eleanor the Harpist (1275–1336)

Christy wrote: "Sometimes I feel as if I'm inside the person looking out, and sometimes it's like a cinema screen watching things
happen to a person I know to be me. When I was the harpist, I was
looking from the point of view of being in the body, looking down
at my feet. That was one experience. I'm sure I saw myself in the
same life, on my travels as a minstrel, looking at myself from the
outside." In our first session, which was not tape-recorded, Christy
first reported being a harpist in the "twelfth" century. In fact the
dates she gave, both in that session and in the recorded session,
described a life that was lived from the end of the thirteenth cen
tury into the fourteenth.

*

In the transcripts that follow, editorial explanations are clearly
marked. In common with most past-life regressions, the client's
language is in modern English, although some unusual words and
verbal constructions do sometimes creep into the responses. The
narrative is printed throughout with Christy's responses in *italic
script*.

*

(Hypnotist) Let's go back to the time when you told me that you
were a harpist. Tell me about your childhood in that life. As I count
from 5 to 1, go through the door and enter the time when you were
a harpist, and find when you were a girl. 5-4-3-2-1.

(Christy) *My mother was a maid to the queen; a handmaiden. I didn't know my father. She never spoke of him.*

Where did you live?

In the castle. It was in England.

In what year was that?

(Christy hesitates) *The 12th century* (then corrects herself) *1283.*

So you grew up in the castle. Who did you have to play with?

Scullery maids' children, kitchen people's children.

What games did you play?

Played hide and seek, in cupboards, behind curtains.

Was that fun? (*she nods assent*) Did you ever do anything naughty?

Broke a pot. It had flowers in it.

Were they angry with you?

They didn't know it was us.

How old are you now?

Eight.

Do you have to work, or can you just play the whole time?

I have privilege. (smugly)

Do the scullery maids' children have privilege too, or do they have to work?

They have to work at cleaning things.

Do they work long hours?

They can play.

Do you play inside and outside?

Inside.

Are you allowed out at all?

We are, but only with an adult. You have to cross the moat.

Which county is that in?

North.

North England? Is there a town nearby?

We are the town.

What is that town is called?

(Christy's initial answer was: *Barren.* Later identification was *Berwick*, a castle in England on the border with Scotland.)

Who's in charge of the castle?
> *The King.*

The King of England?
> *The King* ... (perturbed)

Do you know the name of the king?
> *Sire.* (In a later session she said *Edward.*)

Does he have many people who live with him? Does he have a wife and family?
> *He has a wife – they've no children. He gets angry with her because she can't give him a child.*

What is your name?
> *Eleanor.*

*

Eleanor, take me forward a few years now, please, to when you're twelve, and find out what you're doing. Is that a special time for you?
> *I'm bored.*

Why are you bored?
> *I'm having my lessons. I'm learning my letters.*

Can you write? (*nods assent*) What do you write with?
> *A quill.*

What other lessons do you have?
> *Adding.*

Do you read?
> *Have to read back.*

You have to read back what you've written?
> *I'm just starting.*

Do you learn with anyone else?
> *Just me.*

Do you learn anything besides reading or writing? What about sewing?
> *I knew how to sew anyway; I fix things. I mend things when I sew.*

What sort of things?
> *The curtain we ripped.*

Do you work with clothes? (*nods assent*) Whose clothes do you work with?
> *Mine.*

Does your mother teach you? (*nods assent*) Anybody else? *The other handmaidens.*

When do you learn music?
> *Soon; Mama says if I learn my letters, she'll teach me.*

Does your Mama know music?
> *She plays the harp.*

Did your mother grow up in the town? (*shakes her head*) Where did she grow up?
> *Far away – she doesn't speak about it.*

*

Look forward to the time when you had your first music lesson. Tell me all about it.
> *I'm thirteen. Mama stands behind me at the harp; I sit on the block, she puts my fingers where they should be, and sometimes she tells me to put my hands down, and she plays and then I repeat. Beautiful harp.*

What does it look like?
> *Tall.*

Do you know how many strings it has? (*shakes her head*) How do you know which notes to play?
> *Mama tells me.*

How do you know which tunes to play?
> *I've heard them all my life. I know them all.*

Do you know their names?
> *Some of them.*

Can you sing them?
> *I don't sing, but I listen.*

Do they think you're good at [playing] the harp?
> *Mama thinks I will be.*

How long does it take to learn the harp?
> *I don't know, I've just started.*

*

Let's go forward a year and see how you're doing – you're now 14.
How are you doing with the harp?
> *I like it – play every day.*

Do you meet anyone when you play the harp? Or do you always
play it at home?
> *The queen wants us to play it in the court. There are always people
> in the court.*

Have you been to play in the court yet?
> *Not yet.*

How many tunes do you know now at fourteen?
> *I make them up.*

You're good at making up tunes?
> *I prefer it.*

Can you describe what you're wearing, and what you look like?
> *Dark hair, long and straight ... blue robes and slippers.*

Are they decorated? (*shakes her head*) What's the material?
> *Rough ... Mama says I am lucky to wear blue because it is special.*

Are you excited about playing in the court? When do they say it's
going to happen?
> *Soon.*

*

Shall we go to that time – you're just about to play in the court in
about half an hour ... how old are you?
> *Fourteen. The King likes it. I stopped for a moment and he told me
> to keep playing. There're lots of people, courtiers.*

What are they dressed in?
> *Rich robes ... they are important people ... there's a banquet.*

What are they eating?
> *Chickens and hogs.*

Do you have anything to eat?
> *I will later.*

How long do you have to play?
   Three hours.
Do you have to repeat some of your material?
   I'm making it up.
Are you the only musician, or are there others?
   Just me.
What happens when you stop – do they thank you?
   The King releases me. Then I go and eat.
Were there any young men in the court? Did you notice any of
them? (*nods assent*). Did you have any favorites?
   They're all busy.
You've played before the King. You do this several times, do you?
   I do it every day in the court.
Is your mother pleased with you?
   She is, but she's sick. She's got a fever … she gets better.
Is she still a handmaiden to the Queen?
   She is, until the Queen dies.
How does the queen die?
   She dies in childbirth. I have to leave. The King is distraught.
   Mama has no job.

*

What are you going to do?
   I am going to go away. I walk to the North.
Is your harp with you?
   No. It's too big.
Are you all alone? (*nods assent*) Is it summer or winter?
   It is autumn. I have robes – they're brown – and a bag with a
   small harp, the size of a plate.
So what are you going to do?
   Just walk.
Isn't it dangerous? Walking through the countryside?
   I know how to look after myself. I stop at inns; it's where I meet
   my band.

Tell me about your band.

We are four minstrels. They play a lute, drums, a pipe.

What are their names?

Haldor, he plays pipe; Bob, he plays lute; Peter, he plays drums.

Does Haldor come from that area? That's an unusual name.

He talks funny.

Which inn did you meet them in?

The Tickling Monk.

Where is that?

It's on the border of England.

Where do you go, into Scotland or England?

Scotland. We head for Edinburgh but we never made it – we went to Perth instead. It's nicer there.

How long did you stay there?

I stayed there for ever.

So you settled in Perth with the band?

They kept going.

What happens to the leader?

There was no leader.

Was there a tragedy?

Not a tragedy, but it was sad – unrequited.

What do you mean?

They had to go away. He wouldn't listen to reason about anything we said.

Who was that who wouldn't listen?

Bob, the lute player. (Her tone says that Bob was special to her)

What did Bob look like?

Tall. He was very proud of his skin. He had a warm skin. A pelt.

How old are these boys?

In their twenties.

You are still fourteen?

I'm eighteen. (proudly)

Did the boys want to go to bed with you?

Not the right boys.

In the band?

Not the right boys.

So you didn't let them?

The one I did want, didn't want to. That's why he left.

That's why Bob left? Because you wanted him?

Yes.

But he didn't want you?

He would after the mead.

I see. So you never went to bed with him?

We did, and then I left. (She may mean that she left the band once Bob had gone.)

What happened to you after you left?

I went to a farm. In Perth(-shire).

And what were you doing there?

I tended the sheep. John, the farmer, hired me. He was older than me.

Was he married?

No.

How did he come to have a farm?

It was his father's. He died defending the farm.

From whom?

The bad folk.

So tell me about the farm, and John, and what happened there.

I lived there for the rest of my life. I became John's wife. He was a sweet man, gentle. He made me a harp. Very skilled. We had two children, a boy and a girl.

What were their names?

Eleanor and Simon.

You smiled when you said Eleanor.

It is my name.

Tell me about her.

She was beautiful.

Did they stay with you on the farm?

They wanted to leave. There was trouble.

What sort of trouble?

Stirrings.

Tell me about it.

Bad folk. The bad folk from the North. But John and I defended the farm.

Was Simon there when you defended the farm?

Simon stayed, but I sent Eleanor to my mother.

Did Eleanor get married?

She did, but she could not have children.

Whom did she marry?

A young lad. I didn't like him very much.

What happened to Simon?

Simon stayed until the trouble passed.

Where did he go?

He just left.

And you never saw him again?

I think he did come back, but it was too late to see me.

Tell me what life was like on the farm.

I had to keep warm.

Was it very cold there?

It was open, but part of a valley, so there was shelter.

What was the date now?

'Tis late now.

And you are old, are you?

I must be getting older.

And you are well?

I am well.

And how long do you live after that?

'Til I was 61.

And you lived on the farm? (*nods assent*) Did you keep the bad folk off the farm?

They didn't come back.

Were you happy with John? (*nods assent*) Did he die before you?

He lived longer than I.

Why did you die?
> *I was sad. I knew Bob was gone.*

You never forgot – the whole time?
> *I heard he was gone.*

Did you ever meet Bob when you were on the farm? (*shakes her head*)

You loved him all your life. (*seems distressed*) Are you crying?
> *I didn't cry.*

*

Ok, so let's go to your last day, the day you go. Where are you?
> *In bed. It's dark. I'm just so tired.*

Is John there with you? *(nods assent)* Tell me what happens when you die.
> *Just stop seeing. I* (her spirit) *sit in my chair and watch. I'm looking at myself lying in the bed. I watch John. Then I cry. He's so sad (because) I've passed.*

What can you see now?
> *I look small. I follow John outside. He takes me down to the river. He wraps me up, and floats me out to sea. He sinks me in the river.*

Is that what they do in those parts?
> *It's what I asked him to do. We come back to the farm. He doesn't know I'm with him. But I can't get into my house because I don't exist anymore, so I just wait outside the house, in the field, our field in the valley. I don't know where to go.*

How long do you wait?
> *Winters, summers – a long time – years.*

Does he come and go?
> *I can't see him anymore.*

What happens after that?
> *I got blown away.*

Where are you blown to?
> *Stillness – to a place of stillness. It's good. I go Home. I just wake up. It is as if I've been asleep all that time.*

What is it like at Home?
   Bright. It is still. It's all around me.
Anything else?
   Just bright. I can't make out shapes or distances. It's warm, soft.
Do you hear anything?
   Whispering voices.
Can you make out what they are saying?
   I'm not supposed to; I don't need to.
How do you feel?
   Content.
Are you there a long time?
   There is no time.
Do you think about your past life?
   I don't think at all – not in the way you think as a human.

*

What happens next, Eleanor?
   I'm not Eleanor. I'm no one.
You are in existence. What sort of person are you?
   I'm no one yet.
How do you become someone?
   When I felt it was time.
Did you ask someone?
   I asked myself. I just decided that I should try again.
Did anyone help you make that decision?
   It felt like there was someone there. But they had no form.
Who do you think that might have been?
   A helper – it was just a feeling.
Do you think that helper is with you in this life?
   Not consciously.
And the helper gave you advice?
   It was persuasive. Told me I was ready.
How did you make the next arrangement?
   It suddenly was. The light grows dimmer. Being born: I felt drawn.
   I knew it was time. I was a little boy, Franklyn.

Christy's Comments

An independent spirit, Eleanor is close to her mother – the identity of her father was a mystery. I believe she goes on her travels because she is searching for something, possibly a new outlet for her music. Music is a door to her. Her wanderlust is fueled by her musicality. Maybe she was seeking out musical companions, whom she finds with her band. She also finds love with Bob. However his wanderlust outdoes her own, and where she would like commitment, he desires freedom – the open road.

After the pain of this abandonment, she seeks security and finds that stability with her husband, John. There is not the same passion in her heart for John as for Bob, but John is devoted to her, and they live a happy life.

Before she dies, Eleanor hears word of Bob's death, and she gives up after this. There is a deep sense of confusion when she dies; possibly she feels that she betrayed John at the last – her resignation revealing that part of her heart which never forgets Bob.

Peter's Comments

Christy's chronology was interesting. She did have difficulty in clearly identifying the town where she lived as a girl, but described the lord for whom she worked as "The King." When we re-visited these issues later, her answer led to a surprise. She had previously mouthed the sound "Br..." twice, uncertain of the place name, and then said the name ended in something like "-wich." She also clearly stated that the name of the king was "Edward." My immediate thought was that this was pure fantasy, but there is a slim chance that it might not be so.

These are the historical facts: King Edward I of England stayed for many months at Berwick Castle, which is situated on the border of England and Scotland. He lodged there for the long, drawn-out diplomatic negotiations which ended in 1292 when he selected John of Baliol over Robert the Bruce as the future king of Scotland. On 28 November 1290, in another part of England,

Edward's queen, Eleanor of Castile, died after giving birth to her fifteenth child, Blanche Plantagenet, who died the same year. King Edward I did have one living son, the physically weak and effeminate Edward II, who was born on 25 April 1284. In 1290, when Prince Edward was six, he was betrothed by his parents to Princess Margaret of Norway. The little girl died, probably of sea-sickness, while crossing the North Sea to be with her intended family.

Research suggests that Berwick Castle's governor was Sir Robert Boynton, and its Constable was one of the scions of the great Percy family, Sir Archibald Douglas. Other names current at that time for these two positions are Sir Robert Abeton and William Bisset, Esquire. I can find no record of their spouses, and whether any of them died in childbirth during the period.

My best guess remains that Christy's king was King Edward I, but his wife Eleanor, their baby Blanche, and the weak Prince Edward, who was Eleanor's only remaining son, were dimly and inaccurately recalled, perhaps because the prince had been left behind in London. Edward I, the "Hammer of the Scots," was a powerful and ruthless monarch. It is possible that he had taken a dislike to his weakling son and wanted a stronger one. Or having already seen his three other sons die young, the king was just as hungry for male heirs as his later successor Henry VIII is reputed to have been. In any case, Christy's childhood memory of Eleanor – which I am sure she did not research in advance – is appropriate if not dependable.

Eleanor's given name would have been popular following the marriage of Eleanor of Castile to King Edward in 1254, just twenty-one years before her birth. Earlier in the twelfth century, Henry II's wife, Eleanor of Aquitaine, had established the popularity of the royal name in England.

Other details to be checked were the names and instruments of young Eleanor's band. Pipes (not necessarily bagpipes) were common, as were the lute and drums. Eleanor's own harp was in common usage, according to Chicago-based early music historian and leading lutanist Gail Gillispie. There was also a pocket version of the instrument, the size of a dinner plate, currently in use. The name Haldor may strike us as unusual, but it was also popular at the time. A Scandinavian name, it was a variation of an Old Norse word meaning "Thor's Rock." On the east coast of Scotland and the northeast coast of England, Scandinavian trade and interchange was very common. Haldor the piper was probably a Norwegian or Dane, who spoke with a pronounced accent.

Two things stand out in this account that tie in with Christy's present life as a young jazz musician with a big wanderlust:

First, as a harpist, she was taught by her mother to improvise. She learned some tunes but found ease in improvising melodies that were very acceptable. She showed she had deft fingers in playing her instrument by ear, rather as Christy does today when playing the piano or guitar in the same manner.

Second, she took off alone from the village of her childhood, apparently quite fearlessly, meeting up with a group of musicians on the way. This life, Christy has done it again, by setting off alone from Britain to work in America, almost as if she were replaying the experience. Are these similarities part of a pattern of her life? We will return to that question later on, but we need to keep track of it, as we continue of her soul's journey through time and space.

Eleanor's quiet death on the farm ended a fulfilling but rather wearing life. Dying she seems to have had no concept of what to do next, and her spirit hung around the little farm, presumably until after her husband John had also died. The report of her inter-life experience is vague but has certain commonly observed themes. Home has the characteristic of being brightly lit, comfortable and warm, with quiet whispering sounds. It also totally lacks one feature of life on earth: "There is no time." I chose to make the inter-life experience a minor part of this first session and did not press her for any further details.

At the time we made these recordings, Christy had never read a book on past-life regression, nor concerning psychic awareness, nor about New Age philosophy. Her lack of connection to such literature was a feature that we decided was a real advantage in recounting her journey. We only talked about her reported experiences and how she felt about them.

During this session, Christy usually answered my questions quite taciturnly. Whether this was a physical characteristic of Eleanor the harpist or resulted from Christy's newness as a regression subject was difficult to evaluate at the time. Her story was a little unusual but broadly believable. There was no special magic tale that might be thought to have been deliberately concocted by her, because she had no advance notice of the direction of my questioning. The dating she spontaneously came up with worked well. The unexpected reference to royalty turned out to be both difficult for her to have imagined beforehand, given the paucity of historical information available, and remarkably relevant when my research brought up genuine historical possibilities.

After this first session Christy always rapidly took herself deeply into trance, having discovered her powerful ability to do so. She certainly proved to me many times the old saying that "All hypnosis is self-hypnosis."

2
Franklyn of Lille (1341–1348)

Christy spelled Franklyn's name this way.

How old are you?
> *Five.*

Where are you now?
> *Home.*

Is it a big house or a small house?
> *Small.*

Which country are you in?
> *France.*

Which town?
> *Lille.*

Are Mama and Papa there?
> *Maman.*

What is her name?
> *Elouise.*

Is your father at work? (*nods assent*) What sort of work does he do?
> *He farms. Tills the field. It's not our farm.*

Whose farm is it?
> *The man.*

What is his name?
> *We don't talk about him.*

*

Let's go forward to when you are fifteen.
   I never was fifteen.
Tell me how you came to die then.
   I was sick.
What with?
   Fever.
How old were you?
   Seven.
Do you know what year? (*shakes her head*) Say whatever comes.
   1–3–4–8.
When you die, is your Maman there with you?
   Maman died (after me).
How about your father? Did other people die?
   The whole town.

*

What happened next?
   I was whisked away (with) Maman.
Wonderful. What did you say to Maman?
   We didn't speak. We held.
Where did you go?
   We walked. In the stillness.
Was there anyone else there?
   Many people were there. Maman could not stay long. She had things to do. She said it was all right.
Do you know Maman in this life?
   She's my friend Ruby.
What happened after Maman left you? Are there other people?
   I can't see them.
Are they happy or sad?
   Happy.
What did you think while you were there?
   I rested.
Did you think about your past life?
   I thought about a lot of things.

*

Which is your next life – how did you decide? Were you asked?
I was shown.
What were you shown?
The way out. They just suggested the way out of the place.
You found yourself in a body? (*nods assent*) What was the child's
name?
Saera.

Christy's Comments

Poor though little Franklyn's family was, he lived a fairly untroubled life until his death. Given the voracious nature of the disease
that killed him, one would assume an unpleasant end, but I recall
little of his demise and believe it was relatively swift and not very
traumatic. He was the first of his family to die, which spared him
the anguish of watching his parents succumb to the plague, though
by then they had contracted it. His mother died shortly after him,
to be followed by his father.

Peter's Comments

The Black Death, also known as the Bubonic Plague, is one of the
deadly diseases that fleas can spread to human beings. The fleas
drank the blood of infected rats and subsequently infected human
beings. The Oriental Rat Flea (*Xenopsylla cheopis*) was the cause of
the Black Death in Europe that lasted from 1347-1351. The plague
spread to the little villages of Flanders in the marshlands around
Lille in 1348, which was the very same year as Christy's reported
date of Franklyn's death.

The Black Death came in three forms: bubonic, pneumonic, and
septicemic. Each killed people in a vicious way. All were caused by
the bacterium *Yersinia pestis*. Bubonic plague was the most commonly seen form of the Black Death. Overall, the mortality rate
was from 30% to 75%, but frequently whole villages, both humans
and animals together, perished from the disease. Franklyn was a

French boy. This spelling of his name was current in England and came from the Middle English *frankeleyn*, meaning "Freeman." I have not been able to trace any French usage. His mother's name, Elouise (or Eloise), was probably chosen in honor of the eleventh-century saint of that name.

3
Saera and the Order (1412–1478)

Christy spelled Saera's name this way.

My name is Saera.
Where do you live, Saera?
In a big house in Cornwall, near Bude. (S.W. England)
How long ago?
Hundreds of years. (Later she said her dates were 1412 to 1478.)
How are you dressed, little girl?
I'm wearing a black dress with a hood and slippers.
Where are you now?
I'm walking around inside the house. I'm hiding.
Do you have brothers or sisters?
We're a big family.
Are you playing a game? Who with?
With myself. Mysterious.
Is that what you like to be?
Sneaking around.
What do they say?
They say I'm willful.
What do they mean by that?
That I won't be told what to do.
Do they tell you off?
They can't.

Why?
> *They're scared.*

So, your father doesn't like them to tell you off?
> *My father isn't here.*

Who else lives in the house with you?
> *Many people.*

Tell me about them.
> *They try to protect me.*

Are you someone special?
> *I don't think so; I'm like anybody else.*

What are they protecting you from?
> *The spirits.*

What are the spirits like?
> *Shadows.*

Are you frightened?
> (*shakes her head*) *They're mine.*

*

What happens to you next?
> *I run away. I find a boat. It's big and smelly.*

A fishing boat?
> *It carries goods.*

Does it have many masts?
> *A big mast. There are rats.*

How old are you now?
> *Sixteen.*

Where are you going?
> *To the next port in Ireland, Wicklow.*

What do you do there?
> *Pay them for the ride.*

Are you on your own or with your family?
> *On my own. I ran away because they didn't understand me.*

Are you a little strange?
> *I'm like anybody else.*

You're just independent.

They thought I was special.

What did you do in Ireland?

Wandered around.

Is that safe?

They can't hurt me.

Does anyone try to hurt you?

People tried to hurt me, rob me.

What did they rob you of?

They didn't. They tried to.

Did you have money? (*nods assent*) What else did you have with you?

Just my stick.

Did you find somewhere to live?

I found work in the kitchen of an inn.

Do you like it?

It will do.

What was the name of the inn?

The Grey Eagle. I had to move on; got into trouble.

What sort?

I was supposed to be beaten.

Why beat you?

'Cause they think I'm different.

Did you run away?

I walked away to the mountains.

Where?

Under an overhang. I sat there for days.

Did you have any food?

Just what I had stolen. Needed to think. Confused. I don't know why people treat me like that. They say I sound like a man.

Describe yourself.

Black hair. Thin, hard, pale, strong.

Did you leave the overhang?

I had to go home and face the spirits. I waited for a ship.

How will you pay?

Stow along. Hide away. Always been good at hiding. They didn't see me.

Where did the ship go to?

Back to Cornwall.

Which part?

Same one I left from. I walked and walked. I was tired. I hadn't slept. I rested on the way. They found me before I got home. Said they'd caught me. They thought I'd been there all along. Didn't know I'd been anywhere. Thought I was hiding in the shadows. They thought they knew me!

You were frightened of the shadows?

No.

Were they?

They were frightened of me.

They thought you were a witch?

They called me many things. Sorceress. Beast. But never to my face; they'd never dare. They think they can control me.

Who?

The Order – men and women. Protectors. Priests.

In a church?

More like a fortress.

What did they call it?

The fortress? It was the coven.

Were they regular priests?

They didn't follow the usual patterns.

What did they call themselves?

The Order.

Did you grow up in the Order?

They found me, raised me, or kept me.

Do you know who your parents are?

I think one of ... I never knew.

You think you knew your mother?

I think she was one of them.

Can you guess who your father was?
There were many rumors. No one ever knew the truth.

*

Saera, what happened next?
The test. I have to face them. It was difficult.
What do they make you do?
I had to erase the shadows.
How?
Had to find the light.
Tell me how that was done.
Like a spell – anyone could do it. I passed the test.
I don't understand.
More a mental challenge. Cleanse me of the shadows. So they couldn't take corporeal form. They thought the shadows came from me.
So you drove them out.
I had to do it. I felt better. Brighter.
Had you had the trouble all your life?
No. I never believed them. I believed in the shadows, and I believed they were there. But I didn't believe they were from me. But that frightened me after I passed the test, because they were. I drove the shadows out of me.
What else do you remember?
I was very tired. Had to rest.
Are you still sixteen? (*nods assent*) How long did you rest?
Weeks.
Then you went back to work?
We traveled, all the Order and me.
Where did you go?
All about the countryside, teaching people. That they could help fight. They didn't like us. Mostly they told us to go away.
Did you have enough money?
We were rich. A benefactor who was a merchant.

Did you meet the merchant?
  I did.
What was his name?
  Raymond Black. He traveled around. He gave us the fortress.
Where did you travel?
  South of England.
How long for?
  Not long – not very successful. We went back to the coven and tried to regroup.
Did you have any special friends? Men friends?
  No. They always spoke to me differently. I thought I was like everyone else.
  But after the test I felt different.
Better or worse?
  Both, because I finally felt different. Like I really wouldn't fit. But I felt better because it was true.
What was your daily life like in the coven?
  We would pray. Heal people who came to us. We'd help them. Sometimes we would fight – mostly recreation.
What was your part?
  They mostly looked to me for direction.
You were quite young.
  Eighteen.
How old were they?
  All ages.
You were a sort of leader?
  I was never called a leader.
You were more intelligent?
  They trusted my instincts.
Was there any music in your life?
  Pipes. I like pipes.
Did you play them? (*shakes her head*) Dancing?
  Sacred dancing.

Where outside Bude were you?

Near trees. It would take me a day to walk it – near a stream, very beautiful.

A deep stream? Did you wash in it?

There was a well.

And your clothes?

Black robes. I also had dresses under the robes.

Did you stay long in the coven?

All my life.

How long was that?

A good length.

Any children?

No.

You were in charge of the coven in your twenties?

I was always in charge of the coven.

*

Take me to your death. How old were you?

Almost sixty. I became sad. I was weak and sad. I seemed to shrink.

Was the coven still there?

Yes. We had grown to forty people. Until then they tried to help. Didn't know how to. I had just come to an end. I was tired, drained. Getting dark.

Can hear people chanting.

What are they chanting for?

Speeding me.

You know you're dying? (*nods assent*) Is someone looking after you?

Paul, he's with me; he was wise. My eyes are closing.

You're still in your chair?

I'm so tired. I feel heavy. I've already let go.

Is there anyone in the room?

There're people looking after me, but I can't see them anymore.

What happens?
It's over. I felt like I was falling, falling.
Did you actually fall? (*shakes her head*)
I had just died. In my chair.
What happened next?
They burnt me. They burnt me and I fell. Speeding. Tumbling. Falling very fast.
Are you frightened?
No, it's exhilarating.

*

What does it look like around you?
Dark – neutral. Doesn't hurt. I feel like I rolled over, then I landed.
Warm or cold?
Warm.
You sound surprised.
I'm not surprised.
Why not?
Because it's familiar.
Where are you?
Feels like moss, spongy-light. Like a glow. Being enveloped; it's like light.
If you look down can you see yourself?
Can't see anything of myself.
Can you hear or see anybody?
Not yet; there's no one here, but I don't feel alone. There's a presence. But I can't hear anyone. Nice.
Think about it; tell me more.
The glow pulses like breath … sweet … cushion. I lie down in it thinking about Saera.
What are your thoughts?
She did the best she could. I'm proud of her.

Did she have problems she had to overcome?

She had to come to terms with herself and her burdens – to carry others and their beliefs. But they were her beliefs, and she knew she could do it.

What was the nature of her beliefs?

That she was a protector. Like a conduit for energy. She could channel people.

She was psychic?

No. She could channel people's energies.

What else were you proud of her for?

She never complained for not having a normal life. She just got on with it.

Was the coven a good one?

It has grown.

Did they do good things?

They did.

Was she part of that?

She was. She would pray. It was very physical. Sometimes it was a form of exorcism. She could command the spirits.

Did she make any mistakes?

No really big ones.

Does anyone (at Home) help you think?

The pulse helps me by bringing order to my thoughts.

How long do you stay on the cushion?

Not too long.

*

After that?

I sit up. It gets brighter. Felt like I was falling through the earth. But then it flipped over and I landed in the safe place. It was dark, warm.

Pleasant?

Nice and small like a small hole. I was curled up, sleeping. Then I was born.

Christy's Comments

I felt that Saera carried the burden of a psychic gift. She was thought to be special among her people, given an ability to communicate with the spirits, and to protect those around her from harmful entities. These protective measures took the form of ritual blessings, lengthy prayer-meditations, and, sometimes, entering into a trance-like state to access the spirit world. Despite being brought up in the knowledge of her gift, Saera experienced difficulty with accepting the responsibility that came with it as she entered adulthood, causing her to run away from the Order. She was facing the challenge of taking on the leadership of her group and could not fully comprehend this, feeling unsure that she was up to the task. Her experiences in Ireland compounded her feelings of being an outsider, negatively in terms of her loneliness, and positively in a realization of her inherent strength. She was physically striking and, when faced with the threat of violence, she was able to impose her presence upon her attackers, intimidating them without having to use any real force. Eventually, she came to the realization that she must return home to Cornwall and face whatever lay before her. After undergoing a mental and spiritual trial of acceptance back at the coven (something along the lines of giving a part of herself over to the spirits in exchange for their compliance to her wishes), she was able to come to terms with her role in life, and even find satisfaction in the good her work did for people.

Saera had a relatively easy passing as she had fulfilled her life-task.

Peter's Comments

The pantheistic *old religion* of belief in the forces of nature and the spirit world remained alive in parts of England for centuries after the establishment of the Christian church. It still proclaims itself today, though it has partly lost its practical helping and healing shamanism in favor of esoteric speculation and the sale of handmade craft goods in such southwestern English centers as Bude and Glastonbury. Nature-based life style and religion, some-times called Wicca, centered on "the wise women and cunning men" in the village who were healers, counselors, and therapists. While today's popular presentation of witchcraft delights in over-emphasizing magic and satanic ritual, it is an inaccurate and unfair historical perspective. In the ancient covens there were early pagan rituals celebrating the changing seasons of the year, and some very pre-scientific views of how the world worked, but in that part of England the Christian church was little different at that time. In-deed the two systems co-existed in relative harmony. I remember in 1975 teaching a class in a neighboring Devonshire rural school, and discovering that half of the boys carried a rabbit's foot to bring them good luck and ward off evil spirits.

The area around the small coastal town of Bude was certainly home to many covens. The idea that the Order to which Saera belonged might have been sponsored by a local merchant suggests it was a socially helpful community in which teaching and heal-ing predominated. It is unlikely that the coven was founded on the tradition of thirteen members; more likely it was a loose-knit community that included itinerants and peddlers as well as more settled folk. The little community's later growth to forty strong suggests a measure of economic success, perhaps in farming.

I have found no parallels of "Saera," as Christy spells the name, but there are many variations to the name Sarah and the spelling "Sera" references Sarah and Seraphina, both Hebrew names. Spell-ing was not fixed in the fifteenth century anyway, so Christy gets the benefit of the doubt. Christy loves crazy spelling!

Saera took a boat to the small fishing village of Wicklow in Ireland which was one of the nearest ports on the Emerald Island to which the boats from Bude, on the north coast of Cornwall, might travel. I speculated openly to her that Raymond Black, the merchant who funded the community and lent them the Fortress, might also have been Saera's father. This might have partially accounted for her special treatment by the Order, but Christy thought that it was not the case.

4
Silvio the Italian Rascal

We started with a reference to our first – unrecorded – session, in which Silvio first was mentioned.

Do you remember the little Italian boy?
I remember his hair.
Let's find him. Tell me what he's doing.
Being smacked.
For what?
Stealing.
How old is he?
Nine.
Who's smacking him?
The baker.
What is his name?
They just shout at me because I'm always stealing, because I'm hungry.
Do you have a family?
My father.
Where do you live?
I live in a shack, like a shanty town.
On the edge of town?
In the thick of it.
Where does this take place?
Roma.

Do you have a mother?
> *Just my father.*

What name did he give you?
> *Silvio. He doesn't call me that.*

What does he call you?
> *(sighs) Anything … Boy!*

You like your father? (*grimaces*) You made a face. Is he good to you?
> *He's OK.*

What's the matter?
> *I know I'm bad.*

Why are you bad?
> *I have to eat. I'm small: they don't see me. I'm starting to like it.*

Stealing? (*nods assent*) You know it's bad for you?
> *I don't think it will end up anywhere good.*

*

Let's go to the next important chapter. Where are you?
> *I'm sitting on the edge of the bed. I'm a man now. Just had sex with the whore.*

How old are you?
> *Fifteen.*

How did you pay her?
> *Didn't.*

What does she say?
> *Said I was sweet.*

Is this the first time for you?
> *Yes.*

Do you give her anything?
> *I give her a peck on the cheek.*

Do you ever see her again?
> *I see her around.*

*

What do you do now you're 15?
I'm eighteen now. Laboring. Carry things. I was a messenger once.
Not very good at that.
Are you happy?
I drink a lot.
What do you do when you get drunk?
Fight. Big men.
What happens now?
I picked a fight with the wrong man. I was punching, but he had a
knife; stabbed me in the belly.
What's it like?
Would be worse if I wasn't drunk. Hurts.
What happens to you?
Passing out. There's a lot of blood.
Does anyone help you?
No. I've died.
And where was that?
Roma.

Christy's Comments

Silvio's chances for survival, considering the circumstances he was born
into, were fairly slim. The lot he was dealt – poverty, no mother and
an abusive father – was an unhappy one, and he was forced from an
early age to fend for himself. He was a lively child, and could at times
be a charming young man, although he considered himself to be darker
than the image he portrayed to others. He concealed a lot of pain and
anger, some relating to his father, and he felt abandoned by his mother,
who had died when he was small. He refused to show his vulnerability,
preferring to hide behind bravado, feeling he couldn't trust anybody
to love him. The pattern of Silvio's life was that of a downward spiral,
starting with his descent into crime. Stealing to survive began as a
necessity, but the older he became and the better he got at his "trade,"
the more he began to enjoy it. It was a pursuit that he knew in his heart
to be laden with doom. As the burden of this inner struggle weighed

heavier and heavier upon him, the more trouble he was in. So he fought to distract himself from the problem, and got into the sort of danger which ultimately fulfilled his destiny, causing his violent death.

Peter's Comments

The name Silvio is derived from the Latin *Silvius*, meaning a forest or wood. Both the annals of history and of our contemporary world are full of stories like this wretched one. Silvio lived in Rome (*Roma* is the Italian name). We made no attempt to record the reception given to Christy when she returned Home after this life.

5
The Stillborn and The Deaf Baby

The Stillborn

Are you a little girl or a little boy?

Little boy.

Are you still inside your mommy? (*nods assent*) What does she say?

She's talking quietly to me. She sounds upset.

Why?

Don't know. She sings to me.

Is she happy to have you?

She wants me. (sighs) She's crying.

Why are you upset?

Someone's hurting her. She's in trouble.

What sort of trouble?

Someone's hurting her.

What do they do?

They hit her. She's screaming. I can feel her holding me.

You're still inside your mommy?

(nods assent) *Something's wrong.*

Do you feel hurt?

I don't feel pain, but I know something's wrong. Confusing. Not warm any more.

Is your mother dead?

Don't know. Not warm anymore. I have to go Home. I don't feel safe here.

How do you feel?
I'm scared. Shaken up.
When you died, how old were you?
Six months.

*

You're back at Home. What are they saying to you?
They're trying to calm me down. They say they're sorry.
Can you see your mother?
No. I don't know if she died.
But you died?
It wasn't safe there anymore.
So your mother was attacked and you died. Do you know who attacked your mother?
Man's voice, sounded very angry.
What did he say?
Said, "It's not mine." Loud.
What do your spirit guide voices say?
They're sorry. They didn't know that would happen. I'm wary; it was traumatic.
You feel angry?
Not angry, and not betrayed exactly, but – I don't know – confused. They build me up.
How?
Peaceful – talk peace to me. I trust them again.
What do they say about the future?
They say I must try again – can't stay here forever. They're right. I feel better.
Will you choose the next family?
I'd like to choose, but I don't know, I think I chose last time, and it didn't work out. I'm anxious. They make suggestions, describe people to me.
Are you with any other spirits?
I think there are other people there – the usual bunch. Some leave when they have to.

The Deaf Baby

Do you know who your mother and father will be?

> *I can see her face.*

Are you born yet?

> *I'm about to be born.*

What's that like?

> *Very difficult. I think maybe I'm reluctant.*

Is that why it's difficult?

> *I think so. I'm the wrong way around.*

A breech baby?

> *I have trouble* (breathing heavily). *I'm very small.*

Are you a boy or a girl?

> *A boy.*

Are you OK? Are you with your mother? (*nods assent*) Are you healthy?

> *No. They love me. I can't hear anything.*

Why?

> *I don't know. My mum's worried.*

Are you making progress now?

> *A little.*

*

Let's go forward six months.

> *There were only four months.*

Then you died?

> *My insides stopped working.*

Did you make them stop?

> *I think so.*

Was it your body or your spirit that was weak?

> *My body was weak, and I gave up on it. They* (the spirits) *seem a little cross, not really cross, but they know I gave up.*

At Home?

> (nods assent) *They say I must be braver than that, and they know I can be.*

You've been brave before.
> *Something feels unresolved. I'm trying to work it out.*

Take your time, work it out.
> (long pause) *I've decided I'm going to be a fighter.*

Great! Will you choose your next life?
> *I want to be a girl.*

Are you choosing your parents?
> *I'm going to do it.*

Let's be born. How are you?
> *I'm OK. I'm small, but I'm OK.*

Have you got a nice mommy? (*nods assent*)

*

Shall we go forward a bit? How old are you?
> *I'm six.*

What's your name?
> *Sophie.*

Christy's Comments

The fear and anger to which Silvio was susceptible were not cleared up by the time of the stillborn baby. Although, to a degree, the abusive circumstances dictated the little one's resulting death, the fetus had no desire to fight and was reluctant to be born anyway. Sufficient recovery time simply had not passed when the miscarriage occurred. In the second child, the uneasiness, and the sense of still not being ready to do this, was felt keenly before birth. This resulted in the infant being sickly and, once again, ready to give up and die.

Peter's Comments

It seems fairly safe to suggest that Christy withdrew her spiritual self from the life of the little male fetus. She seems to have developed an acute sensitivity to her difficulties after Silvio's life, and found the replay of a father's anger and the fighting too much for her. In my practice, I have listened to other clients experiencing distress in utero at what was said in conversation by parents and relatives. It is hard to fathom the means by which communications like these may be understood. I have come to discount the theory that we remember what was said when we were in the womb and later translate the words we have heard, after we have learned to speak. My preference is for the view that the spirit of a fetus receives information telepathically. That appears also to be the process by which communication is carried on at Home, as several of Christy's post-life experiences appear to confirm. Christy truly flunked the spiritual toughness test the second time, and she knew it! She had chosen concerned, loving parents, but still she was unready to accept the demands of the baby's fragility. The fact that he was a breech baby suggests to me that her response was already out of keeping with the life she had just begun. The little boy may also have been congenitally deaf as she reported not hearing anything. Anyway, back Home, Christy had to face her sense of shame at her failure, and make up her mind to do a lot better. Next time round, thankfully, she succeeded in handling the situation very well.

6
Sophie the Evangelist (1665–1725)

Where are you?
   In bed. (coughs)
What's it like?
   It's cold, (coughs) *draughty.*
How old are you?
   Six.
What are you dressed in?
   A nightdress.
What is your name?
   Sophie.
Where do you live? Is it a house?
   Smaller. (coughs) *Stone cottage. There are other buildings around us. Straw outside – muddy – been raining. I can't go outside. I'm sickly. I've always been sickly.*
What kind of illness do you have?
   I'm just weak, bad cough.
Do you ever go outside?
   Yes, sometimes.
Do you have any brothers or sisters?
   I have a sister, Josephine, and a younger brother. He's naughty.
Is your mommy at home? What do you call her?
   Maman.
And your dad?
   Papa.

What is your mother's real name?
 Joan.
Which country are you in?
 France.
You seem to be having difficulty talking.
 I'm very tired. I didn't sleep very well. Maman was up with me.
 She stroked my brow.
Were you always sick?
 It used to be worse.
Does the doctor come?
 He came once when I was very bad.

*

Let's go forward to when something special happens.
 I'm riding.
A horse? (*nods assent*) Tell me.
 Chestnut. Beautiful, shiny. He's not mine, but I'm about to ride
 him (coughs) *He's special. A special case.*
Have you ever ridden before?
 No.
Is someone holding you?
 Louis. It's his horse; he's walking alongside so I don't fall off.
How old are you?
 Fourteen.
Are you better?
 I must be much better to be on a horse. I get better, over time. Louis
 has another horse. We trek around. So beautiful.
Where are you riding?
 Forests by streams, sparkling, so good to be outside. I'll never forget
 how lucky I am.
Is Louis nice to you?
 Yes, he is.
How old is he?
 Sixteen; we have fun.

Is he a neighbor?
Yes.
So you played together when you were young?
No, his family wasn't around then.
What is his last name?
Saroux.
What's your last name?
Petrelle.
What town are you near?
Countryside – northern. I've never seen the city.
Which city?
Paris. I don't think I'd like the city. I like wide open spaces.

*

What happens now?
We're sitting on a hill. Beautiful day. I'm happy and sad. Louis wants to go to the big city. I'm not going with him. I think it would be bad for my health. But I'm sad.
What do you say to him?
We say very little, but he touches my cheek. He seems sad, too. I don't know why he would like the city, but I feel I must let him go and not make a fuss.
Are you in love with him?
Always.
Is he in love with you?
He's unfathomable.
What now?
He leaves. I get very bad moods.

*

How old are you?
Eighteen.
What year is it?
16 … I can't see.
Look at a book where it is written.
1681.

What moods are these?

I become impatient, but I go riding ... clear my head.

Are you getting stronger?

I am.

What do you do when you are not riding?

I sew. Mend clothes for people. Patchwork quilts.

Is that what your mother does?

Mama helps Papa with the farm. We have sheep.

Anything else?

I have a horse now. He's beautiful. Chestnut.

What is he called?

Felix. He has a diamond patch of white on his nose.

And you groom him? (*nods assent*)

*

What happens next?

I feel like I'm being called.

By whom?

By God. I fell off my horse. Fell down a hill. And I was very frightened that I would have hurt myself, but exhilarated at the same time. I thanked God when I came to rest at the bottom of the hill, and I felt like He was calling me, and I must repay the favor (of His) breaking my fall.

How do you repay the favor?

I serve Him – made it my life. I take Felix and ride and ride through the countryside. I talk to people. I'm never quite sure where I'm going, but it's all right. I feel I'm being led. It's enjoyable. I feel protected. We keep going.

For a long time?

Years.

What do your parents say?

They would not choose to stand in the path of God.

You're very religious!

I feel I've come through things, and I know I had help.

Where do you stay?
I stay at inns. When it's nice in the summer, I sleep in fields. Felix is very good. He keeps me safe.

*

Let's stop at a place where you are talking to people.
It's just a small farm. I only really stopped to get some milk. But seeing as I'm there (I talk to them). *They are good folk, godly people.*
Tell me what you say to them.
Usually I would try and bring faith to the faithless, but these people have it, believe it. So we help one another. Talk about our lives. I tell them my story, as I tell all people.
And what is the important part of that story?
When I heard. Where I started to listen. When He broke my fall. They are touched by the story. (she smiles) *I love my life.*
Do you heal anybody?
I wouldn't lay my hands on someone and attempt to channel. I just say words; they are from the heart.
What do you believe about God?
I believe He is all around us, in everything we see. People choose not to see Him and He chooses to hide Himself from some, and reveal Himself when the time is right. I say this because I was not a very religious child. My family had faith…but…but He is always there. He caught me when I fell. I think He is a forgiving God.
Does He have anything specific to forgive you for?
Perhaps my bad moods. I still have them from time to time. I'm not perfect. I wonder how Louis is – I think about him a lot.

*

Go forward. What happens now?
I'm on a boat, a small fishing boat.
Where are you?
Corsica.

How did you get there?

I was on my travels. I was in an inn. I was told of a beautiful place.

Corsica is a long way from France.

I traveled for many years.

Do you speak more than French?

I can pass.

How old are you now?

Thirty-three. I'm quite sad. I'm thinking of Felix. He passed away. He was very old.

When?

Not very long ago, but I've been walking for some time. I wasn't riding him when he was old. I thought I should find other people like me. I'm going to the mission.

Which mission?

The one I was told of by the innkeeper.

Do you go into churches?

Of course; they are sanctuaries.

What happens when the boat gets to Corsica?

Very hot. I have to take my coat off. It's all the way up the hill to the mission. There are children everywhere, beautiful olive-skinned children. I come to the gate. I walk up the path. The sun is setting, and I feel I've come home.

Who is there?

Men, women. (broad smile) *I can already tell they're good people, and I'll be able to do good here. I feel there's a sense of release, as if I will really never see Louis again.*

What do they say to you?

They welcome me.

Do you tell your story?

I do. They tell theirs. They've been there all their lives. They've never seen the mainland. I can't imagine what that's like. People come: sick people, sad people, people who need help.

Do you help in the community? (*nods assent*) What do you do?

We start a school. There was no school before.

Do you know how to read and write?

My Corsican is very poor, but I will learn many things. The children like me because of that. We are all learning together. They think I'm funny when I make mistakes.(smiles broadly)

You look very happy.

I am. I have found where I am supposed to be.

How many people in the community?

I would say a thousand.

And in the mission?

We are small, but we grow. People come. It's in flux. There are twelve, but we have guests and visitors. There's a father.

Do you make special friends?

I'm friends with everyone, or I try to be.

How long do you stay there?

I've found where I'm supposed to be. I never left.

Does anything special happen?

I see many births; for a time I help the women. It was a sad time. Or not sad, but wistful, that I had never taken that route. I feel I have many children though, all over, and a wonderful family, and really that is all that matters.

*

You live there till you are very old? (*nods assent*)

I became tired and sickly. I wasn't unhappy with this. It was just my coming full circle. I hadn't ridden for such a long time. It was inevitable I would start to wither.

How old are you?

I am sixty.

Are you dying?

I think so.

Have you had a happy life?

Yes. It does lead me to be a little cantankerous, but they think it's endearing.

What was the best thing in your life?

Coming through the gate. Feeling home. (dying) *I'm leaving.*

Are they around you?

They're helping me. I've been in my room too long. I wanted to walk down to the sea. Marcus half-carried me down the hill. We sat on the beach and he held me and I went to sleep. It was beautiful. So bright. The sun is coming up. It's warm.

What can you see, Sophie?

Sparkly … waves. I'm leaning on Marcus. Very peaceful.

You're still on the beach?

I'm going to the warmth now.

Are you happy? (*nods assent*)

I had a very good life.

*

Are you dying, Sophie?

I have.

Let's go Home. What's it like?

It was wonderful, bright. The sounds of the waves are voices – now they're my people. They congratulate me.

Where are you now?

In the white place.

Are you with other people?

Maman, Papa, Felix; Louis is not here.

Do you see Louis later?

Not this time.

Tell me about Felix.

I can't see him, but I know he's there. He talks to me like he used to – just looks at me. He's welcoming me. Says he missed me. I want to pat him.

Are you able to?

I feel like I am; he doesn't look like a horse. (looks puzzled) *Hmm, I feel very awake now. Maman's hair is golden. Papa is fat and hearty. I can't describe him, not like Maman. She looks lovely. She's younger.*

How old?
> *Thirty.*

Is Papa the same age?
> *He's older – he's older than when I knew him. I hadn't seen him for many years.*

What do they say about your journeys?
> *They're proud of me. Maman thought I'd sacrificed much, but it was no sacrifice at all.*

Do the (spirits) approve of your lifestyle?
> *Oh yes. They take my cough away. They say it served its purpose, and I shall be rid of it.*

Do they review your life?
> *I watch passages. I go to the beach in my mind. I ride in the hills with Louis. I just think of things and they appear. They say they're going to leave me. I'm going to rest and build up my strength.*

Were your parents sad when you left home?
> *Of course.*

Tell me what it was like, leaving home.
> *Difficult to describe because it was my home, but having known my real Home, it wasn't that hard.*

What made you go on the road with Felix?
> *I felt I was being called; I had to repay.*

Now that you're Home, what do they say about that?
> *Papa envied my adventures, as he calls them. He knows it wasn't a sacrifice for me.*

Because you grew strong didn't you? *(nods assent)*
> *It's what I was meant to do in Corsica. Beautiful children.*

What was their language like?
> *Rustic.*

Like French or Italian?
> *It wasn't too far from my own, more primitive.*

*

Did you choose your next family?
> *I asked for it to be chosen for me. I was quite tired.*

What do you choose?

> *To have a family of my own. I pat Felix. He goes. I don't know where he goes. My best friend.*

Do you have any contact with God?

> *Maybe the light. I feel love, anyway.* (sigh of contentment)

Is it a good feeling in the light?

> *It makes you sleepy after a while.*

What happened next?

> *Got very bright, like I was being woken up. Time to go. I felt drawn again.*

Christy's Comments

The first thing to remember about Sophie is that she was a sickly child. The two baby lives before Sophie were the miscarriage and the cot-death, implying the reasons behind Sophie's ill health were residual issues from the previous lives. Because of long periods as a bed-ridden child, once she had grown strong she never took her health, physicality, or the great outdoors for granted.

Louis represented a great leap in her rehabilitation. He taught her to horse-ride, was a companion to her for several years, and eventually became her first and only lover. It seems they had quite a passionate sex life, though Sophie never became pregnant, leading her to wonder, once the affair was over, if she might be barren.

Her mood swings and violent temper following Louis's departure were born out of frustration and dissatisfaction: she needed something to be passionate about. This period of transition seems an important lead-up to her life decision; had she been happy and contented she might not have been so inclined to venture far and wide, serving God.

Sophie had a satisfying and adventurous life, and it feels that, if she regretted anything, it was not having children of her own, something she would only have done with Louis.

A Precious Moment Remembered by Christy

Sophie and Louis are wandering through a wood on a summer's day. Alongside each of them are their horses, one chestnut,the other brown. The sun is high, and dappled sunlight falls through the trees, warming their faces as they walk. There is a small stream running through the wood, and they stop to let the horses drink from it. It is a peaceful, glorious scene.

They are content to talk or be silent; the forest is a delightful place, full of life, and there is enough to occupy their attention without conversation. When they do talk they tell stories, and from time to time, Louis likes to sing. Occasionally he talks of the city, weaving adventurous tales from his imagination.

They continue to walk through the forest, over the stream, up the bank, through patches of briar and up onto the even forest floor. Flecks of color dot the ground, purple and yellow flowers peeking through moss and leaves.

After a time, they emerge from the forest into an open field. They walk to the edge of the field, where it runs steeply into a wide valley. The view is quite breathtaking, and it seems this is new territory for both of them; they have ridden far from home. Louis speaks to the horses telling them not to go far, he then lets them run free in the valley. As they gallop down the hill, Sophie and Louis sit at the edge of the field eating apples and watching the horses.

Peter's comments

Sophie's life was Christy's clear favorite. She overcame her sickness, except for the persistent cough; she fell deeply in love, treasuring the memory of Louis all her life; she had a deep expression of joy in her conviction that God had saved her in a special way, and enjoyed sharing that conviction with the people she met on her travels. And, like Eleanor and Saera, Sophie took to the road, this time with her horse, Felix, in whose animal affection she delighted. Finally she found her home in the Corsican mission, teaching children, delivering babies, and growing spiritually.

Sophie is one form of the Greek name *Sophia*, wisdom. It is appropriate, despite the unconventionality and obvious risks of her mission in that generation. In Christy's melting pot of lives, Sophie's is a triumphant reminder that things can go very well indeed.

The name Christy gave for the community she joined in Corsica was "Ilia." The russet-red island off the north coast of Upper Corsica, at one of the island's closest points to France, fits closely. L'Ile Rousse is today one of the principal tourist traps on the beautiful coastline of the Balagne region. In 1768, shortly after Sophie died, the Genovese sold the region to France, after which it was commercially developed. In Sophie's day it would have provided shelter for corsairs and been a center for fishing, trading, tending olive groves, and growing wheat. It seems likely that her community did not live on the island itself but fairly high up in one of the hill villages. She also mentioned the name Orly, which might have been a local name for the tower dell' Isola dell' Oro, which the Genovese Office of St. Georges built on the island in the year 1600.

7

Tali the Village Boy (1728–1738)

Did you make the decision (which parents to select)?

They were selected for me. I got very excited.

Are you a little girl or a little boy?

A little boy

Where is this?

I don't know yet; I'm very small. But I was eager, eager to get on with things. And then confused. I wasn't sure, but I think it was a very quick birth.

Where were you born?

In a bed.

Was your mother happy to see you? (*nods assent*) And your Dad, was he there? (*nods assent*) Who else was there?

Another woman. I wouldn't cry. Very hungry. I had some milk.

Then you could sleep?

No. I stayed awake. Mother sang me a lullaby.

What language did she sing it in?

I don't recognize it.

What color is your skin?

Black.

*

Let's go forward. How old are you?

I'm ten.

What's your name?
Tali.
Which country is this?
I think it's Africa.
The name of your tribe?
Mali.
Do you live in a village or a town?
A village.
Any other boys?
No.
What are you doing?
I'm in the field. It's hot and dry.
What are you doing in the field?
Just sitting. Staring at the ground. Cracked – I'm worried. We're very poor. We need rain, Father says. Now I'm back home.
What's that like?
It's like home.
Is it big or small?
Small.
What's it made out of?
Mud and straw.
Are there windows?
There are holes.
A door?
There's some cloth.
How many are there in your family?
There's me, my mother, my father, and my little sister.
Do you have any brothers?
No.
Whom do you play with?
I play with [my sister] *Eela*
Do you play with the other boys in the village?
I'm the only boy in the village.

It must be a very small village. Are there other girls?

Yes. People get sick a lot. The water is bad. We don't have enough to eat.

What do you usually eat?

Grain.

Do you eat animals?

We do. We have to share it amongst one another.

Do you go hunting with your daddy?

I'm too young.

Do the men go hunting together?

They do, but it's a barren countryside. We've been cursed.

What happens next?

A meeting amongst the men. We're not allowed to go. Eela and I have to wait with mother. Some of them are going to try and find a new place.

A new place to live? (*nods assent*) Would you like to go with them?

I would, but I know I wouldn't be allowed. Father says I have to look after the house now.

What's your daddy's name?

Biara.

And your mummy's?

Sowela.

Are they important in the village?

Everyone is important in the village.

Do you see the men off? (*nods assent*) Where do they go?

They go west. (sighs deeply)

Are you sad to see them go? (*nods assent*) How long will they be away?

They said not too long – a month maybe.

When they come back, what happens?

They don't come back! There's nothing to come back to.

They have you to come back to.

No they don't.

Are there any men in the village? Or are you the oldest one?
There's no village.
Explain yourself, please.
(very distressed) *We were attacked by the men on horses. Never seen such big horses. They burnt our village and killed us.*
How do you die?
They slit my throat.
What do you feel as they slit your throat?
I'm scared, and I'm angry, and I've let everyone down.
Do people see what's going on?
It's madness; everyone's running around.
Do they take the women away and the children?
They killed everyone.
What was the name of the tribe that does the killing?
Don't know them. White men.

*

What happened to you?
It's very dark. I'm lost; I don't know where I am. I can't see – can't see anything, can't find them. Cold. I'm worried. I don't know what's happening.
Do you know you've died? (*nods assent*)
I can see the village on fire. Everything! I'm pushing it away. I'm lost; I feel like I'm running very fast, but I'm not getting anywhere. I don't know where I am.
Is there anyone to help you?
I'm looking for them … for them … sat down. Dark, but it's not cold anymore. I'm so tired. (long pause) *I'm calmer now. I feel calmer. Because I feel calmer I can see better. There's a small white spot ahead. Everything's very flat around me. It looks like my land.*
Are you walking?
Trying to.
Are you walking toward the light?
I'm quite close. I'm there now.

Is there anyone there to meet you?

My father is there. But my mother and sister are not. I know he must have died too.

Do you recognize your father?

He looks like my father. I feel like I should have protected Eela. I was the only man; I should have done something.

Why didn't you?

It all happened so fast.

And they were a lot bigger and stronger than you, weren't they? Can you forgive yourself now?

(sighs deeply) Can my father forgive me?

What does your father say?

He cannot forgive himself. He says he left us to that (trouble). He's so sorry.

What are you feeling?

So angry. The spirits keep away – they know I'm really angry. Just me and my father. Feels very empty. Giving me time to grieve.

Are you able to forgive the men?

(vehemently) No. I can't forgive them! I can forgive us, though; it was not our fault. It was senseless.

So it wasn't your fault? (*nods assent*) Do other people at Home tell you it's OK?

It feels forgiving, holding my father.

Does anyone say anything else?

I can't see my mother, but I feel like she's behind me. Stroking my head.

Can you see anyone besides your father?

We both feel guilty. I think that's why we're here together.

But they're forgiving you aren't they? (*nods assent*) Many senseless things happen in the world. What happens next?

It's like I pass out; when I wake up there's no one here. I must come to terms with it.

Who is saying that?

I am – they are.

Who is "they"?

The thoughts, the thoughts.

Are you feeling better now, or are you still carrying your grief?

I'm still carrying it. I'm very angry now. I argue with myself; I won't let go of the injustice. I feel like I want revenge, but I know it's over. It's not mine anymore. I have to let it go.

Wouldn't it be better to forgive them? Isn't that what you're being told?

They won't broach that subject yet.

But they do in the end, don't they?

They let me become more peaceful, but it makes me angry again. If I forgive them then I really have to let it go.

But you do in the end? (*nods assent*)

I'm trying to. Once I do, it's actually really easy.

What do they say it's all about – these difficult times?

It's always boys – the boys have trouble.

(Christy means that when she chooses to be incarnated as a boy she always gets into trouble.)

Do you become a boy for a reason?

Trials – it makes me a stronger woman. The things I do as a woman, I can do because of the trials.

How do you feel about it?

I feel it's a balance, a payoff.

In what way?

I'm sad for the boys – they have troubles – but I seem to benefit from it: I have courage.

What qualities do they want you to work on?

They know I have a tendency to be angry, preoccupied. They want me to try and see things, have perspective. Only comes with experience. They know I'm loyal – they urge me to use that and to be a good friend.

Are you making progress?

Yes.

*

Go forward. What's the next significant thing to happen?
> *Time has passed. I'm trying to be peaceful. I think they want me to try again.*

Do you want to try again?
> *No.*

Will they make you?
> *They know that would be rash. I have to build up courage.*

Do you also have to put the anger away?
> *I do, but it's still there. I act peacefully to myself, but it's still there.*

*

What's the next important thing?
> *I see glimpses of what's next. I think they're showing me, persuading me it would be all right. I am making myself ready. Deep breaths.*

What are you smiling about?
> *It's like I'm going to take a plunge.*

Describe the plunge.
> *Magnetic – I'm drawn to this woman.*

Christy's Comments

The early death that awaited almost all the males in this soul journey was also in the stars for Tali. As the only boy in his small village, he felt a burden of an indefinable responsibility that no child could deal with. He was a seemingly playful child until the departure of his father and several of the men of his tribe, upon which he became pensive and distracted. When the white men attacked, and his tribe was slaughtered, his post-death devastation came from the sense of responsibility he felt to protect his family in the absence of his father. Once again, rage and loss clouded his capacity to rehabilitate himself, and to properly find peace at Home.

Peter's Comments

The modern country of Mali, named for the Mali tribe into which

Tali was born, is a sprawling, landlocked African nation in the northwest of the continent, away from the coast and to the east of Morocco. To the north lie Algeria and Mauritania, to the west Senegal, and to the south, Guinea, Niger, and Burkina Faso. The northern area, around the trading post of Taoudenni, is arid sub-Saharan desert. The town used to be a stop on the trade route from Timbuktu to the Mediterranean coast where traders brought slaves, weapons, and domestic supplies. The indigenous people of the area were nomads, frequently moving from place to place as their animals ran out of food and water. The lighter-skinned Moors and Tuaregs, descended from Arab and Berber tribes, fought with the black peoples who lived in a more settled way on the edge of their territory.

Names are harder to trace to the Mali tribe, but both Biara and Sowela are current in the human family. Presumably, Christy's report of her life as Tali involves one of the more northerly family groups living on the edge of the desert and being subjected to a hostile raiding party of their olive-skinned neighbors.

The most interesting encounter was when Tali and his parents returned Home, angry, guilty, and grieving, following their assassination. They were at first isolated by their fellow spirits but when they had calmed down and had started to re-assess their unforgiving attitude, a stream of positive thoughts helped them to grapple with their distress. We are witnessing the "way station" that Home provides for returning spirits to rest and to rediscover their core values before setting off again. Self-forgiveness is a recurring need that my clients have expressed about this stage. The guiding spirits are consistently forgiving, as we will see later, but their test is that the individual returning spirit must be able to clear up trauma from its past life by rooting out any anger, lack of self-forgiveness, and grief. It is a hard job, and not always successfully done, as Christy showed by her poor handling of her temper when she had been incarnated in the bodies of the two little babies.

8
Laeyla of Leeds (1828–1873)

Christy spelled Laeyla this way.

I can hear a chattering. I'm curious.
Where's the chatter coming from?
*From the walls. The walls are like clouds, cushiony, with voices
on the other side. They're not talking to me. They're talking to each
other. I'm curious.*
What are they saying to each other?
Indeterminate. But they sound happy. They sound excited.
About what?
About the new baby.
Are you the new baby?
I think I am. They just started to speak and I was drawn to them.
Are you going to be born?
Not yet.
What are they saying?
They're speaking to me. I feel warm.
Are they your mother and father?
Mother and Father.
Are they happy to have you?
Very.

*

Shall we go forward to your birth? You're born. What's it like?
Cold.

What do they do to you?

Smack me till I cry. They clean me up and hold me. Mother is cry-ing, happy.

How do you feel?

Dazed – tired.

Do you go to sleep?

Proper sleep. Real sleep.

Are you a boy or a girl?

Girl.

What are they going to call you?

Don't know.

Go forward to when you have a name. What do they call you?

Laeyla.

How old are you?

I'm five. I'm helping mother.

What are you dressed in?

A dress, it's brown.

On your feet?

Slippers.

Anything in your hair?

No.

How are you helping your mother?

I'm carrying the water.

What's your mother's name?

Lisa.

And your father's name?

Brian

Do you have any brothers or sisters?

It's just me.

You are the first child?

They waited a long time for me.

Do you know how old your mother is?

No, but she's very pretty. She's wearing a dress and a white and brown apron.

Tell me about your home.
It's nice and warm. We live on a hill.
Do you know what the country is called?
It's called England.
Do you live on a farm?
We live near a farm.
What does your father do?
He's trading. He has to travel. I think he says he's a peddler. Mother makes clothes and beautiful things, and he sells them. He's gone away. He's away a lot. He goes all over the country.
What's the nearest town?
Leeds.

*

Let's go forward to when you are fifteen. What are you doing?
Walking. Behind the house. I have to clean out the barn.
Is it the same house you lived in before? (*nods assent*) Is your Dad still around?
He's not here, but he is still around.
How's your mum?
She's tired. Tired a lot. I don't know. She can't do as much as she used to.
Do you help her? (*nods assent*) What do you do?
Well, I'm cleaning out the barn at the moment. I milk the cows. And I sew. I have to keep making the cloths.
Is it a special kind of cloth?
They're for decoration. We sell them to rich folk.
Do you know what year this is?
1843.
Are you happy?
I'm happy, but I'm worried. She's very pale. She just sleeps a lot now. She tells me she's all right. She misses my father.
How often do you see your father?
I haven't seen him for some months.

Do you know any other people in the area?
> *A few. I have friends. Elizabeth. She doesn't like me to call her Elizabeth. She prefers Beth. She is our neighbor. She's a little older.*

Any boys?
> *A couple. They're stupid, though.*

Are you going to get married?
> *I hope so.*

*

Let's go forward to see if you are married. What's happening?
> *This is private.*(smiling) *Not allowed to talk about this. Come back later.*

It is a little later.
> *We can come back later.*(still smiling broadly)

*

Is he a nice young man?
> *We are married.*

How old are you?
> *I'm eighteen.*

Any children?
> *There's one on the way.*

Wonderful. Are you still living with your mother?
> *No.*

What happened to your mother?
> *She's all right. She lives close by.*

Have you been married a long time?
> *A year.*

Your husband's name is?
> *Albert. I call him Bert. He's a good man. We live in the town now. We have a shop. It's an apothecary. He runs it. He owns it with another man. He put the money into it.*

How old is Albert?

Thirty-three.

You're eighteen? (*nods assent*) Are you in love with him? (*nods assent*) Do you work in the shop?

No. I don't work. I'm upstairs at the moment. I'm too round.

Is the baby coming soon? Let's go to the birth.

I'm scared of the birth.

Tell me how it happens.

I'm in bed.

Is there a midwife?

My mother came. I'm very tired. It's raining outside.

Is it winter or summer?

Summer, but it's raining really hard. (sighs deeply)

Are you feeling the labor pains?

She's ready to come out now. She's very beautiful. She's so small, small and pink. Albert can come in now. I'm calling to him.

What are you going to call the baby?

We like Beth. A nice name.

Do you have any other children?

No. We try some more but ... (distressed)

*

Go to when Beth is ten. You're twenty-eight.

I'm twenty-nine.

What are you doing?

Breakfast – I'm eating.

Is Beth eating breakfast?

She's being distracted by things outside the window, children playing in the street, but she will eat her breakfast.

Which room are you in?

The kitchen. It's very nice. I love my house. We are very lucky. We moved out of the shop. We have our own house now.

How's your husband?

He's very well. Very busy.

How's your father?
> *My father passed away.*

And your mother?
> *Mother lives with us. I didn't want her alone on the hill. She's getting on.*

Is she better?
> *She seems to be. She looks very small to me now.*

Does she still do her sewing?
> *She does. She makes beautiful handkerchiefs. Beth loves her.*

What is Beth dressed in?
> *A green dress. She loves green.*

*

What happens next of importance?
> *I'm pregnant again.* (sounds very scared)

How old are you?
> *Too old for this. I'm forty-five.*

How long have you been pregnant?
> *I think three months.*

Have you told Albert? (*nods assent*) Is Beth still living with you?
> *Yes.*

You seem distressed.
> *It doesn't feel right. Complicated. It hurts. I'm bleeding. There's no one here.*

Are you having a miscarriage?
> *I'm losing it. I feel very bad.*

You're all alone?
> *Mother will be back soon, I hope.*

Beth is not with you? Where are you?
> *I'm by the table.* (moaning) *I'm bleeding very heavily now. I'm so sorry.*

Is it an accident?
> *Just wasn't meant to be.*

Is it an abortion?
> *No.*

Are you going to be OK?

No. I'm sorry – don't know – I'm so sorry. I'm still bleeding. Albert is crying. All covered in blood. He's holding me. I've died. Albert feels very bad. Thinks it is his fault he didn't find me in time.

Where are you now? (*referring to her spirit self*)

I'm standing right next to him. He's all covered in my blood. He doesn't know what to do. I think he thinks I've just passed out. Then he knows I'm not coming to. I'm so sorry, Albert.

What's next?

Mother comes home. This is terrible. It shouldn't have ended like this. I don't want to go anywhere. I want to stay with Albert.

Can you stay?

I feel like I should go. I think I can comfort him.

Are you able to?

I don't know that he believes in such things, but I think he can feel my presence. He's very lonely now.

Do you stay for the funeral?

I stay upstairs. I won't go downstairs. I just sit on the bed.

How long?

I have to go today.

The day you died?

The day of the wake.

Do you see yourself buried?

No. I just stayed in the bedroom.

What happens after that?

I said goodbye. Tried to kiss him on the cheek. He's just crying. I'm at the bedroom door. I go through it and it's dark. I think it's dark because I'm so sad. I wasn't ready. I'm not moving. I'm just stand-ing still.

Do you have any help?

Not for long. I feel like arms are nudging me along.

Can you see anything?

It's getting lighter. It begins to be easier to walk. Sadness ebbing away. I don't want to go in there. Don't want to end it. But I

know it's too late. When I really know that, I go in – back to the beginning. (sighs) *I'm so sad.* (pause) *I'm in the light place.*
What are you doing?
Having a good cry. They hug me. Stroke me. Tell me to cry.
Can you see them?
I can feel them.
Are they good? What do they say?
They said I had a beautiful family who miss me very much.
Do you know Albert in this life?
Maybe.
Do you know your daughter?
I don't know.
How about your mother? Do you recognize her?
I think so; (laughs) *a little like my friend Rebecca.*
And your husband?
Looks like my friend Ewan.
You feel comforted. Do you talk about your life?
They tell me it will all right. They said I have a beautiful family. No, I led a charmed life.
What happens next?
I'm going to rest until I feel better. I lie down and I dream about my family.
Then what?
I'm lying down. They're with me. They know I'm not ready.

Christy's Comments

After my spirit had had time to come to terms with the losses of the previous life, Laeyla was born, and the general quality of her life was much better than that of the children's lives. After a fairly uneventful country childhood, Laeyla found happiness and security with her talented husband, and she fulfilled the wish, devised upon Sophie's parting, to have a family of her own again. She derived much joy from her family and led a contented adult life. Although her husband was not another incarnation of Eleanor's soul-mate, Bob, and Sophie's soul-mate, Louis, but someone else altogether, she found the stability and fondness of their union a source of great comfort, and the sudden shattering of that union a great shock. Unable to comprehend the reason for her death, a tragic blot on her sunny life, she found it difficult to leave her home when the time came, and the difficulties she had were to spill over into her next life.

Peter's Comments

Christy's preferred spelling of Laeyla's name did not impress me, though it is in use today, mainly in fanciful medieval mystery stories. The name is more commonly written as Leyla, which is a variation of Leila, an Arabic word for Night. But the name occurs (spelled Leila) in Lord Byron's poems *The Giaour*, published in 1813, and *Don Juan*, published in 1824, just four years before Laeyla's birth. However spelled, it might well have been fashionable, as Byron was widely read in England at that time.

Laelya's husband, Albert, could have been an apothecary. According to Webster's 1913 dictionary, an apothecary is:

> *"One who prepares and sells drugs or compounds for medicinal purposes. In England an apothecary is one of a privileged class of practitioners – a kind of sub-physician. The surgeon apothecary is the ordinary family medical attendant."*

Their home was in the City of Leeds, a substantial northern industrial city by that time. The population had topped 100,000 by 1851, and the city, mainly involved in the manufacture of woolen goods, was thriving. They may well have been able to afford a house of quality to live in.

It is difficult to imagine that Laeyla's death resulted from a botched abortion; she truly loved her husband and first child and was a very happy woman. The main possibility of excessive bleeding leading to death comes from a specific problem, ectopic pregnancy, that used to be much more threatening in the past. Ectopic (*out of place*) pregnancy (2% of all pregnancies are ectopic) is still the leading cause of first-trimester maternal death in the United States, although death from an ectopic pregnancy is quite rare today, less than one in 2,500 such cases (CDC report). This may give a clue to the correctness of our analysis. Christy affirmed that Laeyla was only three months pregnant when the miscarriage occurred.

What happens is fairly straightforward to explain. The woman's fertilized ovum (egg) implants on tissue other than the intended endometrial lining of the uterus. In 95% of all such cases, instead of the fertilized ovum moving down the fallopian tube into the womb to develop there, it remains trapped in the fallopian tube. The fetus continues to grow inside the tube, which it can cause to rupture or to become severely damaged. Far less commonly, a fertilized ovum can implant in the ovary, abdomen, or the cervix. Eventually, as the fetus grows, it will burst whatever organ contains it. This can cause severe bleeding and endanger the mother's life, even as early as the end of the first trimester. Since an ectopic pregnancy can never develop into a live birth, in the nineteenth century maternal death would be the common result.

9
Peter Boyce the Conscript (1897–1915)

What do you see?
An eye – mirror – shaving.
What are you shaving with?
Blade, a barber's razor; doing a very good job.
How old are you?
Fifteen.
What's your name?
Peter.
Where do you live, Peter?
England.
When?
1912.
You're quite young to shave.
Old enough.
Of course. Do you go to school?
Too old now anyway. Done with that.
What are you going to do today?
Go to town.
What do you do in town?
Nick off. (steal)
Where are you going this morning?
Said I'd go and meet my friend John.

What are you going to do today?

> *Go and find girls. He's a chicken. Never wants to do the fun stuff.*
> *He thinks it's fun to nick sweets. I'm done with that.*

What are you interested in?

> *Girls. Fighting.*

What are you saying to him?

> *Just trying to get him to do something else. He doesn't want to get*
> *caught.*

Who by?

> *Well, you know. His mum's always in town. He's younger, should*
> *be in school. Anyway, my mum don't care.*

What's your mum's name?

> *Elizabeth – Liz.*

Is your dad at home?

> *No, Dad went off. Didn't wanna fight. They said they wanna take*
> *me, but (*pauses*) I wanna go, but Mum wouldn't let 'em. She hid*
> *me. Told them I'd run off.*

Who were they?

> *Men.*

And why do they want your dad?

> *No, they don't want my dad; they wanted me to go off.*

What are they going to do?

> *Going to war aren't they? They think they is anyway.*

What happened now?

> *I don't do nothin'. Try and get into mischief, but nothing doing.*
> *I'm bored.* *

Let's take you forward in time. Where are you?

> *I'm in the big smoke, aren't I?*

London? (*nods assent*)

> *Smells bad. Dirty.*

Day or night?

> *Night. Well, very early morning anyway, but it's still night.*

Where are you?

> *Getting off the train. There's a bunch of us.*

They are friends of yours?

Met some of them on the train, but there's folks from my town.

Why are you here?

We're going off, aren't we?

Where are you going?

Well first off we're going to the coast, you know, but they said we might have to go over. (the English Channel to the war in France)

Who are "they?"

You know, the people in charge.

Did you sign up?

Well, I was signed up more like, didn't have much say in it in the end, but you know, I wanna fight, I'm a man now.

How's the beard coming?

Oh, I still have to shave; have to shave every day now. Got to keep it tidy, that's what they told me. Lots of bloody mustaches here though. Don't like moustaches. They look stupid.

Can you see yourself in a mirror?

'Course I can.

Describe yourself. How tall are you?

Pretty tall. Got blue eyes. Got hairs on me chest. Got stupid hair though.

What sort of hair have you got?

Curly – brown.

Why is it stupid?

Never does what I want it to do. Just sticks up.

Are you in uniform yet?

Yeah, they gave us it on the train.

So you haven't had a haircut yet?

Not yet.

What are you joining, the army or navy?

Army.

Where are you going?

I told you, we're going to the coast first, but I think they're gonna take us over.

What's the date?
> *February the twelfth, 1915.*

Who's your commanding officer?
> *Wrightly.*

What's his rank?
> *He's an officer.*

Don't you know the difference between officers?
> *Well, I'm not an officer.*

What sort of officer is he? Captain?
> *Nah, he ain't that high up.*

You don't know what he is?
> *I only just met him.*

OK. What do you call him?
> *"Sir!" ... I reckon he's a sergeant.*

*

What happens next?
> *We're off the train and we're waiting. In a tent, lots of us.*

In England?
> *Yeah, we're still here. Near Dover. Barracks. They shaved me head. It's very short.*

So you don't have curly hair anymore. How do you feel about that?
> *Well, never did much good anyway. Was weird though, seeing it on the floor – queer like. I don't care.*

So it's February?
> *Bloody cold.*

What do you have to eat?
> *Soup. Everyone's grumbling, but, you know. Gotta keep morale up.*

What do you do all day?
> *Cleaning.*

What are you cleaning?
> *Well, I'm cleaning toilets 'cause I back-chatted Wrightly. We were training with guns.*

What sort of guns?

Rifles.

What kind?

Well, they ain't a Smith and Wesson anyway. That's what me dad had. He had a nice gun.

Do you know what happened to your dad?

I was wondering about that the other day, actually. Thought I might bump into him. Doubt he'd recognize me though; it's bin a while.

*

How long have you been in the army now?

Six months. Got into a fight.

What about?

Ah, nothing in particular.

Whom were you fighting with?

Some berk from the regiment. Thinks 'e's smart. Picked a fight with the wrong bloke, I tell ya.

Why?

Bad mouthing me, that's all.

Is he your rank?

Yeah, but he mightn't as well be, useless turd. Still, I punched him and I got in trouble, so they put me in the clink. Told 'em, it's a bloody waste, do some good. Did the kid some good anyway. Didn't bad mouth anyone anymore.

Did you hurt him?

Not really.

Did he hurt you?

Tried to, but I'm tough. I only smacked him around a little bit. Gotta learn 'em when they're young. My dad did anyway.

Did your dad used to hit you?

Gave him some mouth, you know.

Where did your dad grow up?

He's a Londoner.

Is that why you talk like a Londoner?

Well, he used to take me down there. I liked it.

Did you live in more than one place?

He liked to move around, but my mum didn't so much.

What did he do for a living?

Not a f--- lot, if you'll pardon my French.

What's your last name?

Boyce.

Peter Boyce. Middle name?

Nope. He never saw no need for it.

Your dad's first name?

Arthur.

He's a private in the Army as well?

No, I don't know where he is; I thought I might bump into him, that's all.

Have you written to your mum?

No.

Can you write?

Sometimes, I can write a little bit. She writes to me and you know that's nice.

Do you have any time off?

Well, yeah – I'm in the clink now. Seems I smacked him up a bit too much.

When you had time off, what did you do?

Kick a football around maybe.

You didn't go into town?

Nah, Dover's not got much in the way of entertainment.

How long do you stay in the clink?

I was in there a week in the end.

*

What happened next?

(Long pause – deeply upset)

Where are you?

Sitting on my bed.

What's gone wrong?

Old Mum's dead; she got sick. I'm going home. Going home to bury me mum.

Are you at home now?

I'm still in Dover. I just got the news.

Take the train will you?

Yeah, they said they'd drive me to the station. Been pretty nice about it, considering.

Were you still in the clink when they told you?

I was still in, but they let me out now. Gotta go.

*

Let's take the train. You're home.

Day of the funeral. They didn't tell me till a couple of days after she died, and I don't see how that's right, but anyway.

You arrived in time?

Yeah, just about.

What happened?

We gotta go to the service first. My dad never showed up.

Do you have any brothers or sisters?

Nope.

Does your dad come home?

Don't know where the old git is.

Is it just you arranging the funeral?

Mum's sister, Poppy.

Who comes to the funeral?

Folk from the town. They liked her; she was a nice lady.

Where was she buried?

In the churchyard. Proper gloomy place as well. Raining. Couldn't even stop raining. God!

What happened now?

We have a wake. Got properly sauced. Stupid bugger, made a right arse of myself. She was trying to tell me, but … ain't no stopping me when I've had a few. Fair trashed the place, pretty much.

You just went wild?
> *I'd 'ad too many hadn't I?*

And you were upset.
> *'Course I was. Bloody Dad never showed up. Poppy had found him as well. He'd written her a letter. And he still didn't come. Got me riled up. Couldn't help it.*

So you got drunk at the wake?
> *Most people left anyway. Just as well.*

Do you go back to your barracks after that?
> *No.*

What do you do?
> *Mooched around mostly for a little while.*

Don't they want you back in the army?
> *I'm on compassionate leave. What I said, they were pretty nice about it, considering. I will have to go back, of course. Gotta look after stuff though.*

The house?
> *We had a little house. She owned it now. There's a shop. Sweet shop. Poppy's got a lot of stuff, so she can't look after it. I gotta find someone to look after the shop or I won't have nothing to come home to, will I?*

What happened? Did you find someone?
> *Couple of girls came in. Said they could look after the place, but I don't want no girls running my shop, not unless a bloke's in charge.*

What do you do?
> *I found some geezer.*

Did you know him before?
> *No, he's not from round here.*

Where's he from?
> *Won't say. Goes from place to place apparently.*

Can you trust him?
> *Seems all right. Poppy said she'd keep an eye on it anyway.*

So is it time to go back?
> *Almost.*

Anything else happen?

Well, I had to get myself in shape again. I sort of let myself go.

Doing a lot of drinking?

A fair bit. Polished off half the liquor cabinet. Well, mum wasn't much of a drinker – she had a lot though. I was looking pretty rough. Grown a proper big beard though. Got to get rid of that. They don't like that in the army.

How do you get rid of it?

Shave it off with the same razor.

Is there anything special about the razor?

I think it's my Dad's, cause it ain't my Mum's. But it's my razor now. Think I might take it with me. Crappy, the ones in the army. I made a bloody mess of this though. Cut myself all over. I sort of had the shakes. Probably still drunk. Cor, a right mess. Patch it up all right though.

Are you going off?

No. I'm sitting on the bog. Cor, it ain't 'alf dirty in here. I let it go. It's rough. I feel very sick. I think it's because I've been drinking too much, but I feel very sick. All hot and bothered. I feel queer. Sort of hot, fevery. (moans) Bumpy, sort of bumpy.

Bumps coming out?

Sort of unnatural. Like a shaky, shaky sort of itching. I think I should be sick. Can't be sick. I'm over the bog. Maybe not, maybe that's not it. Sweating. This bathroom's not right. It's dirty.

Are you cleaning it up?

I can't. It's making me sick. There's something wrong. Something wrong about it. I can't move though.

What's making you sick like this, do you think?

Dunno. Feel scared though.

Because you feel so bad?

Yeah, I think there's something wrong.

Is there anyone else in the house?

No, it's just me.

What happens?

> (coughs) *I feel all churny; tummy's churny.*

Are you being sick?

> *No, nothing in there. Just booze.*

Is it the mixture?

> *Nah, that was last night – I pissed that away long ago. Oh!* (sighs)
> *I don't feel as bad.*

Is it passing by?

> *Nah, no, no it's worse. It's gross. I am sitting down.* (moans) *My*
> *hair on my legs is crawling. So, so much. My head itches, cause it's*
> *all short hair, it's all new and sweating all buckets. I feel … I feel*
> *… I feel sort of mad. Not right.*

Is it poison?

> *I dunno. I feel gripped though … gripped.*

Who do you feel gripped by?

> *In my head. I feel weird in my mind. My head's thinking strange*
> *things, like my hair, my hair, my hair. I don't like my hair. And*
> *I'm hot and itchy and it's bumpy, and I want it to get off.*

What do you think it is?

> *I dunno, but I'm scared.*

Look down at yourself. What do you see?

> *I'm bright red. And bumpy.*

Where are the bumps?

> *All over.*

You've come out in a big rash?

> *Oh God! What Mum … it's what Mum … all over. They wouldn't*
> *let me see her, they said she was all bumpy, didn't look like her.*
> *There's something wrong with me.*

Are you going to go and get help, or are you going to stay there?

> *I feel … I'm just staying there. I've scratched them all. Made 'em*
> *bleed.*

What is it?

> *A nasty bloody rash. A mess.*

*

Take me forward.

*They come looking, but I wouldn't let them in. They think I scarp-
ered.*

Who came?

Blokes.

Army?

Yeah.

What happened to you?

Hiding. 'Cause I'm a right bloody mess.

Because of the bumps?

They're sores now.

What do they call the bumps?

They don't call it nothing; I ain't seen anyone.

What do the army do?

*They went away, I didn't let 'em in. It looked like no one was
home.*

You've been there a long time?

*Dunno. (distressed) I found Dad's gun. Can't hold it though,
shaking too much. Not cold though, considering. Bloody hot. Still
thinking weird things, but part of me is   I feel bloody awful.
I was gonna end it. No girl in her right mind would look at me
now. Bloody mess.*

So what do you do next?

I shot the mirror in the living room.

You shot the mirror.

Over the fire; glass all over the floor now.

What happened?

*Sat down. Sat down at the kitchen table. Feel all stiff. Naked.
Covered in sores. And then I did it, I just did it. Bloody did it!*

What did you do?

Shot myself in the side of my head. All over the floor.

What's all over the floor?

My head.

*

Where are you? (*assuming death*)
> *Standing by the kitchen table.*

Does someone come?
> *I dunno. I got out of there pretty sharpish.*

Where do you go?
> *Out the back door.*

Where after that?
> *It's dark outside the back door, didn't look like the garden. Very windy, I'm cold now.*

Where are you?
> *Feels like a void.*

What are you saying to yourself?
> *I'm not Peter anymore – just me.* (voice is much calmer) *I'm still scared.*
>
> *Just want to keep going – I'll get there soon.*

Where will you get to?
> *Out of the void.*

How are you getting out of the void?
> *I have to keep walking. Wind dies down.*

Is it light or dark?
> *Getting lighter ahead.*

You're walking.
> *I'm slowing down now. I'm very tired. Walking for a very long time.*

How long?
> *I don't know. There is no time here. It's getting warmer.*

Can you hear anything?
> *In the distance; I'm not there yet, though. I think there're people up ahead. I think they are people that I have known. I can't see them.*

Do you recognize the feel of them?
> *Yes.*

What are they saying to you?
> *They're talking amongst themselves, because I haven't arrived yet. I think I'm eavesdropping.* (laughs)

What are they saying?

Comforting words. Their words are more like an action than words with meanings. They say something and I feel as if I have been hugged. It feels safe. I'm in amongst it. It's nice. It's Home. It's bright and warm, and people are part of the walls, and it's moving in and out like a pulse, like a heart.

Do you know the people?

Parts of them are me, and parts of them are other people, in the same way that I would be part of other people's hearts. It feels wonderful.

Do they say anything about the life you just lived?

I was very anxious. That I'd done such a bad thing that I would be punished. They said my journey was all the punishment I needed. People are not punished, they punish themselves. I cannot properly have forgiven myself.

Can you now?

Maybe I can. Maybe I can't.

Are they telling you to forgive yourself?

Until I untie myself it will not come to be. They tell me to be patient and forgive. But they remind me that I can take my time.

But haven't you now forgiven yourself?

I have forgiven myself for the deed. But as long as I act in the same way I'll never let it go.

What is the problem you have to face?

Self-destructive. Greedy. Indulgent. Cowardly. Irresponsible. They tell me I must amend these ways by being patient with myself and not being quick to judge.

Who says this?

The people in the walls.

Are you going to follow their advice?

I'll try to.

Can you ask for help?

That's a very good idea. They say they do help me and they are always with me.

Ask now.
> *Show me how. They said they will help me if I need them.*

Can you learn your lesson now?
> *I will try to.*

What is the lesson?
> *Love yourself.*

And do you?
> *I do.*

Christy's Comments

Peter was as difficult and rambunctious as the rest of the boys. However, where Silvio had insight into his own situation, and Tali was self-aware, by comparison, Peter was immature and ill-prepared to handle life's obstacles. He had the lazy, irresponsible attitude of a drifter – a quality he might have attributed to his father, had he been more attuned to introspection – but he was not without his good points. He truly loved his mother, although he was somewhat too defensive to communicate that in her lifetime, and was distraught after her death. That Peter's own death was by suicide reiterates the "give-up" tendency of the males, although, to be fair, he was not rational or even completely sane at the end, but feverish and disfigured, facing an unhappy life, or another violent death at war. Peter was a lonely soul who seemed at odds with the world, dissatisfied, but unprepared to do anything about it.

Peter's comments

During World War II, bombs dropped by Hitler's Luftwaffe destroyed ninety percent of the records of World War I military enlistment. Thus it was not possible to have the easy confirmation of Peter Boyce's undistinguished military career that I had taken for granted when the recording session with Christy came to an end. Peter's roughneck life is not the stuff of history books, though his violent death may have been recorded somewhere; our details are just too sketchy to give us clues. Peter's mother may well have died of measles; there was a sudden spike in measles-related deaths that year, as an epidemic traversed England. This would account for her coffin being sealed from Peter's view. He could have caught the disease in the military prison, on the train, or from infected people in the town when he returned home for the funeral. I considered the possibility that the rash that frightened him so much might have been smallpox, but there were no deaths in England and Wales from that disease during that year. I suspect that a severe outbreak of measles was enough to frighten him into thinking he had smallpox, and his massive consumption of alcohol so deranged his thinking that he took his own life in a panic attack. There was little to live for; after all, he would have been shipped out as cannon fodder to Yprès or the Somme, had he returned to the army.

His father's gun, which he used to commit suicide, could have been made by Smith and Wesson, an American company founded in 1852 with a world-wide reputation for craftsmanship and strong sales in Britain before the Great War. In the Light's "way station" Christy grappled again with her need for self-forgiveness, helped on by her comforting spiritual mentors.

While Christy sometimes used specific words or phases reminis cent of former days in her descriptions, the only time she consistently spoke in an accent was for Peter Boyce. For a while, because her London brogue was so strong I thought she was making up the story. My attitude changed as I observed the real distress she felt at times, which showed in her facial expressions and her body movements. Whether the accent is authentically 1915 I do not know. In general hypnosis subjects speak in their normal way, as Christy did even for Franklyn, Sophie, Tali, Joyce, and Hector.

10
Joyce the Housewife (1928–1978)

Joyce's life was immediately before Christy's, and it ends with a time of agonized reflection "in the warm place." We were following the lead of a small but lifelong outbreak of eczema that Christy has suffered, that brought us straight into a dramatic incident.

What are you doing?
> *I'm cooking.*

What is your name?
> *Joyce.*

How old are you?
> *Thirty-four.*

What is the year?
> *1963.*

What are you cooking?
> *Boiling water in a pan. It catches in my sleeve.* (very distressed) *I burned myself. All down my legs and arms. Burning.*

What are you doing?
> *Screaming. Words. Bad words.*

Are you alone? (*nods assent*)
> *I run to the bathroom, to try and immerse myself. Can't fill the bath quick enough. My skin's bubbling. Peeling. I pass out next to the bath. Black.*

Someone comes?
> *He came and found me.*

Who came?

> *My gardener. He picked me up, put me in the bath, with water on me. It wakes me up. I'm crying.* (still very distressed)

Tell me how you feel. Where does it hurt you?

> *Everywhere. Everything hurts, feels crazy. He's in my house – why is he in my house? He helps me.*

Don't you know this man?

> *He's my gardener. He's a quiet man. He's not allowed in my house.*

Does it matter? He's helping you.

> *I know he's helping me. Saying quiet things to me. Calls an ambulance. Goes downstairs to use the phone.*

Tell me about that.

> *I don't know; I'm in the bath.*

What happens? Are you in your clothes?

> *Yes. I get out of the bath, try to;* (very perturbed) *my clothes are sticking to me now.*

Where does it hurt the most?

> *My legs – up my thighs, my arms. I start to black out again. He comes back.*

Are you lying down?

> *I'm sitting on the floor, leaning on the bath. Scorching waves of pain are shooting up my body.* (crying)

Is the ambulance coming?

> *Yes. He sits with me, keeps me calm. Tells me the ambulance is coming. I say he should go before it gets here or he'll get in trouble.*

Why would he get in trouble?

> *Because he's in the house.*

Who cares? Who says so?

> *People.*

Why do they say that?

> *Because he's a Negro.*

What country is this in?

> *America.*

Do you send him away?

I don't want him to go. He's keeping me calm, but I don't want him to get into trouble. He waits with me until the ambulance gets here. Then he goes out the back door.

Tell me what happens when the ambulance gets here.

I break down. They pick me up. Everything hurts – never stops hurting. I feel like I'm going numb. (distressed) *Blacked out again.*

When you come to, where are you?

In the ambulance. The nurse doesn't see I'm awake. She's looking at my legs. I black out again.

Is that because of the pain?

It makes me sick, sick; my legs feel like they're bubbling. Then they go hard and shiny, and my skin peels off. Disgusting. I feel like I want to be sick. (distressed) *My head feels like it's going to burst. Hot, so hot, going up my head.*

How long does it take to get you to the hospital?

I don't know, but it feels like an age. Takes so long to get there.

What happens when you get to the hospital?

I pass out.

And when you come to?

I can't feel anything. They've given me drugs. Everything's got ointment on. Shiny. Putting bandages on me.

Which hospital?

Rogers … something.

Are you there a long time?

A few nights. They change my bandages, but they have to be careful; it pulls my skin off. But I keep the ointment. I apply it myself.

You come out of hospital. Who's at home?

I live alone. I take it easy. My friend Suzy comes to stay with me. I lie on the couch. Watch television. Read.

What do you read?

It's my book I'm writing.

Are you very clever?
> *I never went to college.*

*

(At this point I thought it was therapeutically necessary for Christy to re-live the trauma of the kitchen accident. The re-examination brought out some further details.)

*

You need to go back to the kitchen. This time you'll feel no pain. I want you to describe it.
> *I wasn't paying attention to what I was doing. My sleeve caught on the handle. I was looking out the window into the garden. And I was punished.*

You were punished?
> *And the water spilled down my legs and onto my arms.*

Can you see it? You don't feel any pain.
> *I'm watching it happen. Things slow down. I bruised my arm from knocking the pan away as it fell. It was just boiling.*

Do you go to the bathroom?
> *I tried to use the sink in the kitchen first. Too high up, but I was screaming.*

Somebody heard you.
> *Joshua was in the garden.*

He came in, didn't he?
> *He heard my screaming, came in to see what had happened.*

A good man. Go forward to after this is all over. Next time you meet with Joshua, what do you say to him?
> *We don't talk about it. Pleasantries.*

You didn't say anything more than that?
> *We didn't need to. He had a hard life.*

You were kind to him?
> *I try to be.*

Why did you say the pan punished you?
For looking at Joshua
Do you find him attractive?
I'm not supposed to.
Do you find him attractive?
Of course I do.
Is that what you thought – that the pan punished you?
*It's what I thought as it happened. I didn't think about it any-
more.*
How long did you carry the scars for?
Rest of my life. I never wore skirts again.
Looking back on that situation, what do you think about it?
I think I was stupid.
It was an accident. Can you forgive yourself?
Just should have been different.
In what way?
*It was bad time. A difficult time. So much hate but I never did
anything about it.*
Who were your parents?
Bill and Theresa.
Did your parents have a black gardener?
No, they died.
What did they say about black people?
My Dad said some things – but my Mom was open.
What did you think about their opinions?
*They were from a different generation. I thought Dad was wrong,
but I didn't blame him for it. Maybe I should have.*
So you felt guilty?
*I never helped. I was never mean or rude, but I should have done
more. I felt more guilty because I had privileges they didn't have,
and there was no reason for it. I just wanted to be equal. I would
have been happier to let my status drop.*
Tell me about the book you are writing.
It's just a diary really.

What happened to it? Did you ever publish it?

It was for me.

Did you do a job, or look after the house?

I never had to work. Paul, my husband, left me a lot of money.

When did you get married?

I was young.

*

Go back to your wedding day.

I didn't feel very much – a little nervous maybe, but I already knew I didn't love him. Still, I looked very pretty; I had a beautiful dress. My Dad looked very proud.

How old were you?

Twenty.

How old was your husband?

Forty-two.

What sort of work did he do?

Had a construction firm. (He worked) in the office.

Was he the manager? (*nods assent*)

Bossy and rude. Stressed.

Did you have any children? (*shakes head*) What happened to the marriage?

He died on our tenth anniversary. He got drunk and drove his car into a tree.

Were you in the car?

No. I had got out and walked. We had a fancy dinner, and I was just sick of him, and he knew it. He always drank too much. He drank way too much. We had an argument. I told him stop the car, because he was shouting. I got out and walked.

Walked home?

Went through the fields. I didn't go home that night. So I didn't know until I got home the next day, and they wondered where I was and what had happened. I felt happy, relieved.

Did you see the body? (*shakes her head*) Did the police question you?

> *They did, but I was known in the town. People knew him, knew what he was like. People never thought it was foul play.*

*

How old are you now?

> *Thirty.*

Which year is it?

> *1959.*

After what happened, did you live alone?

> *In our house. Carried on as usual; met friends, went out; I had a nice time.*

Did you have anything to do with music?

> *I like music.*

Did you sing?

> *I was too shy.*

Play piano? (*shakes head*) What music did you like?

> *I liked folk. We used to see things at Robeson's, the coffee shop. Kids would sing and play guitar — it was wonderful.*

Did you have a lot of friends?

> *I had a circle. I didn't like the housewife thing. I think they would say I was aloof. I didn't mean to be.*

But you had plenty of friends?

> *I had enough.*

After the accident, did you dress specially?

> *I always wore slacks, and long sleeves.*

How long did you live?

> *I wasn't very old – fifty.*

Was there anything special between the accident and your death?

> *I felt more peaceful, but I just did the same thing: I wasted my time.*

What happened to the gardener?

> *He went to jail.*

Why?

He didn't do it, he was framed. A robbery. It wasn't him.

Where?

A bar. A seedy bar.

Did you talk to him?

I saw him once.

In jail? (*nods assent*) Before he went to jail, were you friends with the gardener?

He stopped working for me.

Did you have any men friends?

My brother, Jeff. He was younger than me. He lived far away, but he came back after the accident.

Did he live with you?

No he had his own place.

Was he married?

He wasn't the type. (smirks knowingly)

What type was he?

He wouldn't say, but we knew.

You weren't supposed to talk about things like that?

He just liked different people.

Did he have men friends? (*nods assent*) How did you feel about that?

He's my brother and I love him.

Did you like his men friends?

They were stupid mostly. I never really knew them very well though.

Did you take any vacations?

My life was like one big vacation.

You never went away?

I didn't need to – it was beautiful.

Who did you leave the money to?

Jeff.

Why did you die?

I don't know why I did it, I was just bored. I started to drink. I shouldn't drink; I'm not the type to drink. The bored housewife who drank herself to death. Stupid. It shouldn't have gone like that.

What did you think about your accident when you were drinking?

I thought about it, but I didn't think about it. I drank to stop thinking about it. It would keep popping into my head, and I would keep drinking. I never thought why – or maybe a part of me thought why, and the other part of me would drink more.

Did you ever have a relationship with Joshua?

(shakes head) *Drank myself to death.*

*

How? Go to your last moment.

Just passed out. Sitting on the kitchen floor. I was sick, I was lying on my back. Stupid.

Choking?

I was, but I didn't know it – I was passed out.

What happened next?

Felt like I was falling, clawing my way up, berating myself for being so stupid.

Can you see your body?

I can see it in my head, but I'm not there.

Where are you?

In some tunnel. Like I'm inside my throat. Stupid. Very difficult – I'm not getting anywhere. It's futile. That's how I felt about my life. It was futile and pointless. So I just let myself go. (switching to after her death) *I keep falling, until I fall into the warm place.*

Describe it.

My warm place with the light and the whispers; reassuring. Even rock bottom is right back at the beginning.

In the light place, does anybody speak to you?

I have to deal with it myself.

Who says that?

I say that. I'm not alone – there are voices, but I have to deal with it myself.

How do you deal with it?

Like I'm peeling off all my skin and starting over.

Where are you now?

Still in the warm place.

You felt the frustration and hurt has come along with you into your next life?

I did the best I could, peeling off the feelings.

*

Let's go back to the end. You're there drunk on the floor: what are you saying to yourself?

I can't say anything anymore. I didn't know I was going to die. I just thought I was drowning my sorrows. Felt very ill suddenly. But it's too late; I can't focus on anything anymore. And I'm falling over, rolling about on the floor like an idiot. I can think that.

Are you going to take all that grief with you?

I don't want to.

(Christy had brought some of the self-directed anger and guilt over into her current life, so we dealt with that issue therapeutically before ending the session. See the introduction to Hector's life for more details.)

Christy's Comments

Joyce is complex: cold but compassionate; cut off emotionally; immensely disappointed with herself, her life, and the things happening in society. But she recognizes her own complicity in the civil rights mess. She feels guilty for not having the guts to be in the thick of it, where she could do some good. She feels she is a coward.

The pan of water and the feeling of punishment are more about being punished for her cowardice than for her briefly admiring Joshua. It is the reluctance to admire, or the inadvertent shame she feels (possibly because of her upbringing) upon looking at Joshua in physical admiration, that she feels she is being punished for, rather than for actually looking at him.

Leaving her money to her brother is like a little kick in the teeth to her husband Paul, and is done partly for that reason – childishly wanting to take revenge on this man who sucked up the best years of her life with his dull, aggressive (but never physical) behavior. Strangely she doesn't feel guilt about her unemotional response to his death. He wasn't so bad a man. It is more an indication of her psyche being shut down. Fairly tragic things happen in her lifetime, but she responds with, at best, a kind of wary melancholy. Perhaps this is the source of her aloof quality.

Peter's Comments

We had some rather weak leads as to the whereabouts of Joyce's home. As her brother or other relatives may be still alive we have omitted details Christy supplied to safeguard their privacy. I found it rather frustrating that we had a clearer idea of the areas Eleanor and Sophie lived in, all those years ago, than of Joyce's location. There was also some evidence of the information being blocked when Christy visited the Akashic library. Despite our inquisitive need to verify information, we were unable to do so.

More interesting is the clear connection between Joyce's demise and those of Silvio and Peter. All three had alcohol-related deaths. Silvio was asking for trouble when he picked a fight, but he might not have anticipated that his opponent would have a knife and that he would die. In Peter's case binge drinking clearly was a factor in his suicide. He had run out of desire to live in circumstances that his fevered brain told him were desperate. But Joyce was under no such pressure. By her own account she was bored stiff, lonely and frustrated (she could only name one friend and admitted that she was aloof). Yet she had shaken off her horrid husband's memory and she seemed to cope fairly well with the marks of her severe scalding. I truly believe that Joyce did not intend her death. She was seeking relief in the wrong place and of the wrong type. How very human, but how very contrary to the design of her spiritual training. We briefly recorded what happened to Christy when she got Home. Once again the "reassuring" voices of the "way station" call her to come to grips with her problems. Clearly she must have desired very strongly to do better next time, as today's Christy was born just two years after Joyce's death.

11
Hector the Roman Sculptor

One investigation Christy and I had made for therapeutic reasons was not directly related to the idea of tracing a series of lifetimes. As I have noted before, Christy suffered from life-long outbreaks of eczema affecting the backs of her arms at the elbows and around her ears. According to a number of hypnotherapists, this persistent and annoying complaint has sometimes been linked to the carry-over of trauma or guilt from past lives. Another frequently cited example of such energetic carry-over is asthma, which has often been linked to drowning or suffocation in a past life. I thought we might try to see if there was an opportunity for healing by accessing a distant trauma, which might not have been fully resolved in days gone by.

*

There are three essentials for self-healing in hypnosis:

The first is that the hypnotist is not responsible for the diagnosis of the illness. The client's own feelings and self-diagnosis serve best, for the simple reason that it is not the physical body that is being worked with, but the spiritual self and the subconscious mind.

The second essential is that the problem or disease, linked by the client with the past-life experience, may be resolved by letting go of the past hurt and by self-forgiveness. In this case, we started the session that brought back a memory of Joyce's life by making a request to Christy's subconscious mind to take her back to the life that was most closely related to her current eczema problem. At first I supposed that the scalding hot water burning Joyce's arms and legs might be the cause of the eczema (though it did not affect the same part of the body). Then came Joyce's unexpected death, choking in a drunken stupor, and this little exchange took place after she had died and Christy was back Home:

I have to deal with it myself.

Who says that?

I say it. I'm not alone – there are voices – but I have to deal with it myself.

How do you deal with it?

Like I'm peeling off all my skin and starting over.

Although that sounded right, it was a false lead, but I dealt with it therapeutically, encouraging Christy to put an end to the trauma and to forgive herself. The narrative that follows was a replay of Joyce's story in another session.

You felt the frustration and hurt has come along with you into your next life?

I did the best I could.

But this was when you got eczema?

That's what I mean – I did the best I could peeling off the feelings.

Let's go back to the end. You're there on the floor; what are you saying to yourself?

I can't say anything anymore. I didn't know I was going to die. I just thought I was drowning my sorrows. Felt very ill suddenly. But it's too late; I can't focus on anything anymore. And I'm falling over, rolling about on the floor like a f ... idiot. I can think that.

Are you going to take all that grief with you?

I don't want to.

Let's think about it and bring the grief to an end. You've suffered a lot, drunk yourself to death. Now you can stop it; you don't have to take it into your next life. Does someone say that to you in the warm place?

I want someone to say that to me.

Why don't you say that to yourself? You can forgive yourself. Say that.

Let it go!

I'm going to ask you to go forward. Now you're Christy. You made a mistake, but you can forgive yourself. Tell yourself. Tell the woman. Take her in your arms. Tell her it's OK. Say the words:

It's all right. Let go!

Let go of the eczema...tell her.

Let go!

Do you understand, you don't have to have eczema anymore.

The third essential in this kind of therapy is that the client needs to be taken right back to the *very first time* such a problem ever occurred, when her mental attitude to the problem may have been established. Finding this Initial Sensitizing Event (ISE) is of fundamental importance in resolving many difficulties.

Christy's eczema seemed to fade for a while, but it did not go away. Joyce's life was simply not the life that contained the ISE. So which one was? Peter Boyce's life, despite his "bumps," did not contain the answer either. We had to search further, but time was running out because Christy was due to return to Britain for good. We both felt that we already had enough lives – spanning from 1275 to the present day – to justify our research, but we still had not resolved the eczema problem. There was only time for one last session. For this I would again use the "affect bridge technique," involving Christy moving backward in time while holding in her subconscious mind the image or feeling about her outbreaks of eczema.

After Christy had wrapped a black scarf round her eyes, which best helped her to focus within herself, she spent a few moments lying on the settee calming herself. Then she signaled with a finger that she was ready to begin. I led her thoughts down a long stair-case in an underground (subway) station (I suggested London's Goodge Street station, but she replaced that thought with the stairs at Leicester Square station that were more familiar to her). Then we took an imaginary train into the distant past.

When we arrived, at my suggestion Christy got off alone, leaving me to await her return. I asked her where she was, and almost immediately she was assailed by fierce emotion. Her chest heaved and her hands knotted tightly together. At first it was hard to make out what was happening, but after a while the nature of the tragedy became apparent. So I concentrated on helping her to feel deeply but to avoid becoming strongly traumatized, asking her to repeat what she was describing by looking at the scene as on a monitor. (It seems a little incongruous to ask someone experiencing a scene in her past history to view it on a modern TV monitor, but it works!) This technique enabled her to relive the time with greater emotional ease, providing more material from the sad story. Then I recalled what Dr. J. H. Conn had said in *Hypnosynthesis* (1967), that the therapy wasn't really about the memory of a trauma suffered but about how the client had processed it and had reacted to it.

Christy put up no psychological defense against the thought of releasing and forgiving both herself and others involved, so at the end we attempted to put the grief and anger at Hector's life away for good. This was done by "re-scripting" the emotions that were felt previously, a re-telling of the story which sometimes works in the context of current-life regressions but is a bit easier to accomplish in a past-life setting. Would we have success this time with the skin trouble? Or must we reach even further back in time to find the ISE of the eczema at some future date? At the time of this writing, Christy's eczema has faded, but it has not completely disappeared.

A Roman Tragedy

(Christy's premonition was right. Serious trouble lay ahead in a life she recalled which was by far the earliest of them all. She guessed that the setting was ancient Rome, during the period of classical sculpture.)

Tell me what you are doing.
> *I'm in two places at once* (breathing deeply, long pause). *It's a cave.*

Are you alone? (*a great deal of distress was being exhibited*)
> *Yes.*

What are you doing?
> *Cutting myself.*

Why are you cutting yourself?
> *Payment.*

For what?
> *I'm not really here.*

Something bad is happening? (*very distressed and dislocated*)
> *Their hands on me.* (plus incoherent rambling)

*

Let's go back a bit. Where are you now?
> *I'm walking. There are pillars.*

What's it like?
> *It's calm. There's a garden.*

What sort of garden?
> *Rocky – waterfall.*

What are you wearing on your feet?
> *Sandals. Leather sandals.*

What else are you wearing?
> *Robe.*

What color?
> *Cream.*

Are you a man or a woman?
> *A man.*

How old are you?
> *Thirty.*

How are you feeling?
  I feel anxious.
About what?
  I don't know. I just feel agitated.
Are you far from home?
  No. This is my home.
What sort of place do you live in?
  Stone. It is cool. I sleep on the floor.
Do you live with anyone else?
  No.
Why are you all alone?
  My wife's not here anymore. She disappeared.
Do you know why she disappeared?
  I'll pay for this! (still very upset) *I got consumed by my work.*
What is your work?
  I'm a sculptor.
What sort of things do you make?
  Statues.
Which country are you in?
  Italy.
Are you near a town or a city?
  Rome.
What sort of sculpture were you working on?
  I was making a statue of my wife. I just got consumed.
In what way?
  *I confused them. And I neglected her. She sought happiness some-
  where else. I couldn't make her happy.*
Was she younger than you?
  A little younger.
What was her name?
  Epiphany.
And what did she call you – what is your name?
  Hector. (distressed) *I'm sorry.* (distressed breathing) *I'm seeing
  it all happen.*

How did it start?
I found her – and I did away with her.
What did you find her doing?
She was with another man.
So you killed her. How did you kill her?
I stabbed her.
What happened after that?
I hid her body in a cave. They didn't know I'd found her with another man.
What happened to the other man?
He walks free.
So you hid her body in a cave. Is that where you were sleeping?
It's where my mind is.
Tell me what you are feeling and thinking.
I finished the sculpture. There was a … my friends came and saw it for the first time.
What did they think of it?
They found me on the floor.
What were you doing?
Taking my skin off, trying to make a new me. They said a madness took me. (breathing heavily) *I think I am mad.*

*

(At this point Christy anxiously asked to be returned on our special train back to the present time.)

*

I'd like you to stay a little longer. We need to go through this for your sake. Tell me what happened next please. You're by the statue. What are you doing to yourself?
Just bleeding. I tell them about the cave.
Do they go and find the body? (*nods assent*) What happens?
They put me out to sea.

On a boat? (*nods assent*) All alone, or with others?
    All alone.
What happens to you?
    I fell into a darkness.
Are you still bleeding?
    The birds ... the birds found me, but I was gone by then.

*

Before we go any further I want you to go back to the very beginning, but this time I want you to look at it like a television monitor,
as if it is about someone else. You won't feel anything. Let's start at
the discovery of your wife and the man.
    I saw them at the window (calmer) *and a rage took me. I wanted
    to burst in and pry them apart. But I didn't − I stood there trem-
    bling. I felt it important not to be caught, so I tiptoed away. I
    waited for her to finish. He left and I pretended that I had been
    out. Then I came upon her. I'd been working. I had my chisel. I slit
    her throat, but it was messy. Then I stabbed her many times.*
How did you feel as you were doing that?
    *I didn't feel anything − it's as if I wasn't there. That's why I think
    I'm mad.*
What happened after that?
    I wrapped her up in a sheet.
How did you carry her?
    Put her in a cart.
Did anyone see you do this?
    *No − that cart was within my walls. I covered her over; then we
    rode out of town, up to the cave.*
Did you bury her there?
    No, I just left her in the cave.
What did you do then?
    *I came back. People were worried. We didn't know where she was.
    I finished the sculpture of Epiphany.*

*

What happened after this?
Then my friends arrive. They find me on the floor, taking my skin off.
What part of your skin?
My arms and legs.
Any other parts? (*shakes head*)
Just (breath catching) *my arms and legs.*
Can you feel yourself cutting yourself?
I can see it – it's disgusting. A lot of blood.
What do your friends do?
They grab the chisel, take it from me.
What do they say to you?
They're shouting, "A madness has taken him." They try to find out what is wrong.
Do you tell them?
I try to tell them. I touch Epiphany. (the statue) *There's blood on her.*
What happens now? *They understand. They find her. It's bad. I'm not myself anymore; I'm outside of this. I can't help them. I know they must punish me now. I swoon. They're pecking at me.*
The birds? (*nods assent*) So they put you on the boat? (*nods assent*)
Do they give you oars or a sail?
No, they just push me out. I think they think I'm dead already.
What happens after you die?
So dark, so dark and cold. I'm still in the boat. I don't feel mad anymore.

*

Are you a spirit now? (*nods assent*)
Doesn't help though – just makes everything more real. I want to forget everything.
Can you forgive yourself?
I pity me.
Can you forgive the man she was with?
I suppose so.

Say the words.
I forgive the man she was with.
Can you forgive her for betraying you?
She didn't betray me.
Did you betray yourself?
I was uncontrollable.
Can you forgive yourself?
It can't ever happen again.
Can you forgive yourself?
No. I have to know it will never happen again.
Can you stop the feeling passing on from life to life? If you can't forgive yourself, can you release yourself from this torment?
Yes. I want to release myself.
Say the words.
I release myself.
Tell me what happens after the dark, cold place.
The sun rises.
What happens to your body?
I don't know. I'm not looking at it any more.
What do you do now?
I step off the boat into the light. I'm Home.
What's it like?
It's a relief.
What are you saying to them?
I'm not saying anything.
What are they saying to you?
They're consoling me. They're sorry. They don't need to forgive. There's nothing to forgive me for – it's over.

Christy's Comments

It is so difficult to find within myself an adequate comment. Hector lived a very long time ago, and many of my lives followed his unhappy end. In our current life, we all know who we are and what we have done, good or bad. When we find out that we don't like who we are, we can try to change ourselves. But when we are looking at a desperate situation in a past life, change is just not possible. It is locked in as part of our history.

For me, what does remain possible is to try to understand the forgiveness that was held out to me when I returned Home from being Hector. That divine forgiveness was and always will remain a living reality for me, and is the best comment on Hector's life that I can find in my heart.

Peter's Comments

One of the exquisite problems of engaging in past-life regression is that you may turn up something you really do not want to know about. Hector's dramatic end is such an agonizing event. After all that was uncovered in this last session, we did not stay around to discover anything more about his life. Christy had some impression of his good standing in society, but that was all. This was a true crime of passion, with a ring of authenticity about it that was confirmed in the palpable distress Christy showed throughout the whole session. Had I not been using a powerful microphone and a professional recording machine, much of what she said in the first half of the tape would have been lost, as she was so upset and so soft spoken.

The story was itself a classic tale: an artist preoccupied with carving a beautiful statue of his wife forgets to give the lady enough attention. Perhaps he even falls in love with the statue he has made, or so he concludes when he finds her in the arms of another. Maybe the girl was profligate, but he did not think so, because he blamed himself for her infidelity. Hector's emotional distress led on to a brutal, unwarranted but unpremeditated murder from which his sensitive, artistic self instantly recoiled in horror. At first he tried to cover up his crime by hiding the corpse in a cave (perhaps the Roman catacombs), because he could not bring himself to actually bury the body. Indeed, part of his distressed mind stayed with her as he pretended not to know where she had gone and carried on in putting the finishing touches on the carving of her statue. But when his friends arrived to see his work, they found him literally tearing himself apart in a mad frenzy, killing himself in his grief. In a deep coma, and presumed by his friends to have died, he was laid in a boat and pushed off down the river Tiber, or out to sea, where the birds began to feast on his body. It was a gruesome end, but by then his spirit had finally departed. This is a remarkable story, worthy of a great classical tragedy, but it actually happened in the distant past of Christy's spiritual life. If only we could now identify Hector's statue of Epiphany, should it exist among the treasures of ancient Rome!

The forgiveness issue could fill a whole book. Briefly, the evidence we have from the Other Side is that each life we live is a discrete training episode. The eternal spirits live in a dimension of unconditional love where there is no such thing as judgment. Pain, suffering, judgment, hell are all states of mind that belong to the dimension of the planet Earth. So Christy's judgment on her life as Hector is a natural human response, and it is equally natural that she should be received back into the spiritual realm where judgment simply does not exist. (More on the issue of reincarnation in the final chapter of this book.)

12
In The Akashic Library

As our time together came to an end, Christy and I both wanted to clarify some of the details that had seemed less than certain when first recorded. In several instances she had acknowledged she was not entirely sure of this or that detail, so we had deleted them from the written record. Throughout our work, Christy, who had a marvelous recall of what she saw and felt, was also proved to have a very sensitive apprehension of what was true and what might have been just her imagination. On one occasion she began our session by saying she was a gardener in a graveyard, but then quite quickly indicated she did not feel the record was "real." I suggested that we back-track into the present, whereupon I deepened her hypnosis, and she returned to the past, accessing a very different life with which she was comfortable.

It seemed impractical to spend the significant time needed to go looking for details through her past lives all over again, so I decided to take Christy to the Akashic Library to look up her records. This is a well-known reference place on the Other Side, although Christy had never heard of it before. Although I deliberately led her to this place, I did so with minimal suggestions, and her uptake of the library image, expanded with details all of her own, supported the current experience among metaphysical practitioners and my own non-directed work.

This account is reduced in length, because parts of it have been incorporated in the foregoing narratives for ease of reading. There were instances where the Library record seemed more in doubt than our original record, so we made no correction. Absolute certainty of details is simply not a realistic proposition, which is a limitation in this kind of work. Christy, like my other past-life subjects, had a much stronger impression of her thoughts and feelings than any concrete knowledge of dates and places. In some instances it would be foolish to ask for details. We live today in a world of maps, newspapers, and clocks. To ask the little African boy, Tali, whether the sun was high in the sky would be reasonable. But to ask for the exact location of his village might be to court fabrication. This is one reason to seek birth and death dates at the Akashic Library, where, logically, they may be held as reference points. Chronology was also presumed by asking Christy to go forward from one life to the next by turning the pages of her record book. This is how we know that Joyce was the life before Christy's own, because we took her spirit forward from Joyce's death to Home, and then to the next birth where we found ourselves with Christy as a baby, being bounced on her grandfather's knee.

The First Library Visit

> You're outside a big library. There are white pillars. Big stone stairs in a flight leading up to the main doors. It's a long library with people sitting there. You ask to see your book. Tell me when your book arrives. (*pause*)
> *It's here.*

Are you looking at your book? (*nods assent*) Describe it.
> *It's bound – brown.*

Does it have your name on it? (*shakes her head*) What happens when you open it?
> *I haven't opened it yet. I'm nervous.* (long pause) *It's like a picture book.*

Can you see a picture of Eleanor?
> *The places she's been.*

Can you tell me what she looks like?

Long dark hair.

Is there a place in the book where you can check dates?

I could look.

Can you please?

Looking ... 1336 when she died. *

Tell me about Franklyn.

There isn't much here.

How does he spell his name?

He doesn't spell it. (meaning he was illiterate)

Do you know when he was born?

1341.

*

How does Saera spell her name? Can you read it?

*They're manuscripts. I'm trying to see them. They're inside the
pictures. S-A-E-R-A.*

When was Saera born?

1412.

When did she die?

1472.

*

Look for Tali. Where did he come from? Take your time.

Trying to find what his tribe was called. Looking at the village.

What part of Africa was he in?

North – north and east. Not near the coast.

When was he born?

1728.

*

Can you find the record of Joyce? When did she die?

'78 – 1978.

How old was she then?

She was 50.

*

Do you have a favorite life?
> *I like Sophie the best.*

Tell us something more about Sophie.
> *She was very passionate sexually.*

Did she have affairs with men on her travels?
> *Oh no!* (annoyed) *She was never with anyone after Louis.*

Tell me about that.
> *She was just a girl. She needed something to be passionate about. Louis was overwhelmed. I think that is why God showed himself to her. Her temper was bad without something to be passionate about. The irony of her celibacy. She would have made more money as a whore.*

She made love to Louis a lot?
> (guardedly) *In their time.*

But she didn't have a child?
> *No. She often wondered at that. Thought she might be barren. But never found out.*

What was the happiest time in her life?
> *Coming home (to Corsica).*

For a moment look up from your book, and look around you at the Library.
> *It's huge. I can't see where it finishes. There are shafts of light. You can see the dust in the shafts of light. It's exquisite.*

Who is there?
> *Many people, but there is so much room. You can see people upstairs looking for things, as far as the eye can see.*

What do the librarians look like?
> *They look like librarians – with specs on.*

Look around outside the library.
> *It looks like heaven. It's bright, like clouds. It's beautiful.*

Are there any people there? (nods assent) People you know?
> *There would be if I needed to find them.*

Are you happy in heaven?
I don't know that it's heaven, but I like it here. I feel sunny.

The Second Library Visit

What can you see?
Light, sort of misty – indistinct.
Go through the library doors. Take a seat. Look at your book. Can
you answer some questions? (*nods assent*) Is it all writing or are
there pictures in it?
Pictures. They move.
Do you have to turn the pages or can you ask them to turn?
I like to turn the pages.

*

Let's go to Eleanor. What was the name of the lord?
Edward.
Tell me about your band. What were their names?
Haldor, pipes; Peter, drum; Bob had a instrument like a lute.
Did Haldor come from that area? That's an unusual name.
He talked funny.

*

Let's turn to Franklyn. What was their last name?
Lillion.
And the name of the town they lived in?
Not a town.
A village then?
Near Lille.

*

Thank you. There was a long time between Franklyn and Saera;
was there anyone in between them?
It's blank. I think I was at Home.

*

Are you comfortable in the library? (*nods assent*) Are you sitting down?
(*nods assent*) What sort of chair are you on?
A wooden chair.

Is the librarian nice?
They are helpful.

*

Let's go on to Saera. Do you know the name of any village near
the fortress where she lived?
Near Bude – a day's walk.
Is the fortress still there?
No.

*

Let's talk about Sophie. What was the name of the village of her
childhood?
Something "-nay." (long, searching pause) *I'm confusing it.*
Let's find the village in Corsica.
Ilia.

*

What are you looking at in the book?
*Looking at the pictures. Interesting to see the chapters like that.
Strange. Pages look rough, but they're really smooth. They're a bit
like liquid.*
What is the picture in front of you?
A wood. Dappled sunlight. It's a favorite place.
What are you doing there?
I'm walking alongside the chestnut horse.

*

Now we're at Laeyla. Is the farm on a hill or in a valley?
On a hill. Little Hangsey? Something "-sey."
What was your married name?
Roberts.
Where did you live with Albert?
Leeds. Busy.

*

We're on Peter now.
The pictures are clouded with emotion.
Where did he grow up?
Slough.

*

Let's move on to Joyce. Let's go to Robeson's coffee house. Do you remember your friends' names?
Celia. I'm not that close to them.
Are the singers students? (*nods assent*) Which college?
St. Mary's ... seems right.
Why did she drink so heavily?
Bored.
But she hated her husband's drinking
Ironic.
Why did she do the same thing?
I don't think she connected them.
What sort of thing did she drink?
Vodka.
Did she ever drink with anyone else?
She didn't drink very often. Not a drinker. She would have a glass of wine with dinner, but otherwise there were only two or three times when she got really, really drunk.
Quite an accident then?
She just took it too far.

*

Is there anyone you recognize in the library?
There aren't very many people.
Do you have any special friends here?
Not really.

Peter's Comments

Christy experienced a lot of emotional pressure when she visited the Akashic library. It was not an issue of being unable to visualize the place, or to answer my series of questions from the book she was given. There was an emotional tension which resulted in her having neck and back pains and a feeling of exhaustion after each session. Because she was a very good hypnosis subject I believe she "picked up" the fact that some kind of restriction had been placed on our visit, so that we should not ask too many questions.

Some people have learned to access the library records without the use of hypnosis but by prayer instead. However, they are not able to have the sight – as Christy had – of the magnificent building, of her brown book with moving pictures of her past lives, and of the exquisite rays of celestial sunshine pouring down into the space.

One purpose for my including these snapshots of her visit to the library is to show the degree to which we may access information that is individually recorded about our past. The idea of a collective record of the human race, into which we may dip to find our own story, fits in with what Christy saw and with the records she obtained from her two visits. It may be, however, that when the vibrational energy our own individual past-life record does not fit well enough with our current spiritual needs, the Akashic library book may show us a record from another part of the collective unconscious of the human race. But our own personal records, replete with our unique energetic imprint, will normally be the first to emerge. So, for example, Christy's real distress at the tragic story of Hector, and the apparent connection of his death with her current eczema outbreak, suggest strongly that the past life she retrieved was indeed from her individual part of the cosmic records.

13
Recollections of Home

1. The Departure from Earth

Christy's series of lives demonstrated her human activities interspersed with her spiritual experiences. Life on planet Earth is always secondary to the eternal life of our spirit. This is why as soon as she died in each human situation, she continued her narrative as a newly freed spiritual being – the main player in the drama – carrying on with its life. It was as if she had changed from being a caterpillar confined within the hard shell of a chrysalis to breaking out and flying free as a butterfly. As Christy said shortly after Peter Boyce had blown his brains out, "I'm not Peter anymore – just me."

There is a transition from the earthly life, when it is finally over, to the spiritual realm, which Christy (as I shall refer to her spiritual being in this chapter) calls "Home." Then comes the journey from Home back to Earth, when the time is ripe for our soul to take its place in a new human body and to undertake more terrestrial training.

The end of life may or may not prove difficult for individual spirits to understand and handle. Hector seemed a little confused at first, when he died in the boat. It was "so dark – so dark and cold," mirroring the darkness of night, of his death, and of his deep despair. Then the sun rises over the water, brightening his dark spirits. Christy says, "I step off the boat into the light. I'm Home."

Despite her quiet death in old age, Eleanor's peaceful ending caused Christy's spirit some long-term difficulty. She seemed to fully understand that she had died; she just stops seeing. "I sit in my chair and watch. I'm looking at myself lying in the bed. I watch John, then I cry. He's so sad because I've passed." She was quite unwilling to leave her beloved husband. She followed him to the river, where he floated her enwrapped body toward the sea, until the waterlogged bundle sank out of sight. But still she could not leave him. Even though, for some reason, she had no access to their farmhouse, she waited and waited for years until she no longer saw him, presumably because of his own death. Only then, when she had finally grasped that he was no longer around, did she allow herself to get "blown away" back to Home.

Why did Eleanor hang around so long? Was it truly her love for John? Perhaps it was, as she admitted, that she had never really shaken off the memory of her infatuation with Bob the lute player, her first true love. Was Bob her soul mate, or are there no such relationships, despite what people say? Maybe it was a sense of guilt at not having been wholly committed in her heart to John that kept her hanging around the little farm through the many seasons of the succeeding years.

Franklyn had no such trouble – he "whisked away," and likewise, Saera, who followed him chronologically, did not stay around for long. After her cremation she fell (the term was never explained), "speeding, tumbling, falling very fast. I feel like I rolled over; then I landed." As she died in her chair, Saera may have lurched sideways and translated this final sensation into the feeling of falling that bridged her passage from earthly life to Home, the eternal realm of unconditional love and service.

The distressed feeling was true also for the Stillborn child, who was taken home rapidly after losing the feeling of bodily warmth. For the sickly Deaf Baby, however, physical distress was not the only issue. "My insides stopped working," reported Christy, but when I asked her whether she was instrumental in some way in making them stop, she admitted, "I think so. My body was weak, and I gave up on it." There is a little evidence from other past-life regressions that some souls may not care to stay around in weak human bodies, or even in family situations they consider distasteful. When a spirit has left, unless it has been replaced by another spirit – which it is reported can occasionally happen – the physical body of the infant dies. The evidence is clear that no human being will continue to exist outside the womb without a soul attached to it.

Then came Sophie, whose dominant thought upon dying was of the very good life she had just ended. Her triumphant return Home was in no way echoed by Tali, the African boy, whose life came after hers. The poor little lad had been senselessly slaughtered by strangers and reacted accordingly: "It's very dark. I'm lost. I don't know where I am – cannot see anything, can't find them. Cold! I'm worried; I don't know what's happening."

The word "cold" is a clue to Tali's transition at death. He is entering a cold region of helplessness which is very common for those who are murdered or die sudden and violent deaths. His village was on fire, but he was pushing the thought away because he was in denial of his demise. Yet he was slowly becoming aware that more was expected of him: "I'm not getting anywhere," he said, implying that there was an inner purpose to be fulfilled. He may not have known where he was, but he was looking for "them," presumably his parents and sister. Warmth began, at last, to seep back into Tali's consciousness as he gained a greater sense of purpose. He was tired out by the psychic struggle he had been going through, but felt calmer, and because he felt calmer, he said that he could see better.

Here is a commonly noted element of the death experience that we have not encountered so far in our study. It is the vision of a bright light ahead that draws the departing spirit like a magnet. Now Tali could see that the territory he was crossing was very flat, but it looked "like my land." So he walked toward the light until, at last, he was there.

Tali's soul may have been confused on his journey homeward, but Laeyla's soul was very precise in her understanding of her changed life situation. She readily acknowledged her death. Her heart went out first to her grieving husband, Albert, and then to her mother, when she finally arrived back in the house at the death scene. "This is terrible," she cried. "It shouldn't have ended like this." She was torn because she felt that she ought to return Home, but at the same time she wanted to comfort her husband. "I don't know that he believes in such things, but I think he can feel my presence. He's very lonely now." A powerful feeling of concern for those left behind is commonly experienced by the newly departed. However, Laeyla seemed to know her boundaries. She just stayed upstairs, sitting on the bed, until the day of the wake. She did not go to the funeral, but waited until Albert came upstairs, where she said goodbye to him. "I tried to kiss him on the cheek." Either because of her presence, or despite it, Albert wept as she went away through the bedroom door. Then, interestingly, she immediately lost sight of her home and entered into darkness, a darkness caused by her own sadness and regret at her untimely death. She stood there in frustration until, at last, she felt "arms are nudging me along." The atmosphere got lighter; it was easier to walk, and easier to let sadness ebb away. At last she realized that she must put an end to her sad feelings about her past life. "I know it's too late," she admitted with resignation as she found herself "back to the beginning in the light place."

Quite the opposite of this experience was Peter Boyce's story. After he blew his brains out, his spirit dashed away from the scene of his suicide in the kitchen and "got out of there pretty sharpish." Christy knew Peter had made a bad mistake, and her understanding of his faults was like a strong, cold wind as she entered a void. She also knew she was no longer Peter, but approached her new situation with some of his old qualities. Despite feeling scared, she wanted "to keep going out of the void." As she took greater spiritual control of her emotions, the wind of her fears and shame died down and it began to get lighter ahead. She slowed her pace, feeling exhausted by the struggle, and walked on and on for a very long time. Slowly her consciousness picked up the sound of other people, whom she had known in the past, though she could not see them. Then she felt as if she might be eavesdropping on their conversation, because they did not yet know she was there. Still, once again despite all the difficulties, Christy had returned safely Home.

In comparison to Peter's journey, Joyce's transition Home seemed quite rapid. She could visualize her body lying on the kitchen floor, but it appeared to her that she was in a tunnel, like her throat. Here, I suspect, there's a psychic connection with her choking death. Realizing the futility and pointlessness of her life, she had let go. Whether Christy's soul had willed Joyce's lonely death or not, we do not know. Like Saera, she had the sensation of falling until she tumbled "into the warm place, my warm place" with the light and the whispers reassuring her. "Even rock bottom is right back at the beginning." And so it was, each and every time the transition took place, a return to the point of departure.

It would appear from the research literature that our transition Home after physical death depends very much on our prevailing state of mind. Those who are confused after a long life are frequently recorded as wandering around within the confines of Earth in a kind of daze. Sometimes these souls even attach themselves to living people and stay as bewildered hangers-on in a shared environment. Some, unlike Peter Boyce who deliberately made a quick transition, are so appalled by their former life that they feel they cannot or dare not return to the realms of light, love, and forgiveness, which are Home's characteristic spiritual qualities. They may be consumed by guilt, or still involved in thinking and planning evil. For such spirits the transition from the hell of their own making is long, slow, and fraught with difficulties. In the end, we have learned, the only time when hell is a reality is when the soul creates one for itself.

There is an inevitability about returning to the starting place of Home; it is bound to happen eventually. It happens either because of these spirits' dawning understanding of their need for help or, it is reported, through the direct intervention of the Bright Ones, spirits who have an assigned task to rescue the spiritually lost, either by helping them to regain their confidence and sense of purpose, or by reclaiming them from their denial of the way of love. For those who are ready to return, and who know the way there, the transition is a breeze; as Christy said after being Franklyn, "I was whisked away." There is also evidence that practice makes perfect, and that the longer spirits have been coming to earth, the more likely it is that they will take the fast track Home.

2. The Reception at Home

When she finally gets Home, Christy's spirit has various experiences. There are consistent feelings expressed in her reports. For Hector, it is a feeling of relief and the experience of consolation. Eleanor feels content at being back. It is a place of stillness. It is good, bright, and all around her. She cannot make out shapes or distances, but it is warm and soft, and she hears whispering voices that make her feel content. She is not aware of time or of human thought processes; she just is who she is. For Franklyn, Home was represented by the comfort of holding on to Maman and walking with her in silence. Saera finds she is unsurprised to be back in the familiar atmosphere, where it is "like moss, spongy light, like a glow, like light, like being enveloped." She does not feel alone because there's "a presence," but she cannot hear anyone. It is "nice," and "the glow pulses like breath." Sophie declares Home to be "wonderful, bright," and Laeyla finds herself in "the bright place" as well. Even after Peter has fled from the scene of his death, he declares that Home is "Nice, bright and warm, and people are part of the walls and it's moving in and out like a pulse, like a heart. It feels wonderful!"

So the environment at Home is uplifting and encouraging. Christy expresses no reticence or regrets at being there. But what of the reception awaiting her arrival at the "way station," a sort of reception area where newly transitioned souls are received and held? What of judgment and retribution? The tradition of western religion places great emphasis on the idea of a Day of Judgment, and Hector's life raises that issue immediately, but we receive a report that may be astonishing to people who are looking for a verdict to be handed down on one who has clearly broken the Commandments.

What are they saying to you?

They're consoling me. They're sorry. They don't need to forgive. There's nothing to forgive me for – it's over.

Is this the whole story? Clearly, in the condensation of Christy's report, we must accept that much more was said. But the upshot of it all is that, for her, Hector's life has not been subjected to spiritual retribution; rather she is given treatment to rebuild her spiritual confidence and self-forgiveness. And this is the key. Christy's spirit has had great problems with self-forgiveness. Even after eleven other recorded lifetimes and many more uncharted ones, although she was psychologically prepared to release herself from the experience when I asked her, she still held back from saying the word "forgive." Self-forgiveness is undoubtedly the toughest task we have to do.

Franklyn had his Maman to hold in silence for a while, although she left him to do other things. There were other people at Home who, though he could not see them, seemed to be "happy." Christy rests and thinks about Franklyn's brief life "and other things." After her life as Saera, she lies down on a soft cushion, thinking about that experience. Transition is always followed by serious reflection.

The trauma of dying in the womb produces a quite different result for Christy. Here the spiritual world intervenes for her benefit much more obviously than before. The spirit voices say they are sorry, but they did not know things would turn out so badly. They feed Christy with peaceful thoughts until she is in the mood to trust them again. Not so after the deaf baby dies. Here the spiritual mentors set out to help Christy come to terms with her failure to accept the experience as a test of character to which she had committed herself.

Clearly the happiest and most detailed reception of all occurs after Sophie's death. She has had a triumphant life, has lived constructively in willing herself to overcome ill health in youth, and has endured a lifetime of troublesome coughing. She has also resisted the temptations her sexuality brought her, refraining from going into the town where she might have lowered her spiritual standards. She has risen to the challenge of her belief that God had intervened in her life, has forged a solitary but inspiring ministry, and has cultivated a deep and mutually caring friendship with her horse, Felix. Finally, after intuition has bought her to the mission in Corsica, she has used her time well in the service of others both young and old until her dying days. In consequence of her success, perhaps, Christy gets to meet her parents and to pat her old friend Felix, although when she arrives Home she does not encounter her lover Louis. The spirits take away her persistent cough and congratulate her for her lifetime's achievements.

Tali's life ended in his murder. Christy is received by Tali's father when she arrives Home and feels her mother stroking her head. She is aware of forgiveness issues while with her father. The spirits keep their distance from her anger, though they communicate the forgiveness she must begin to feel – both toward her murderers and toward herself for the feeling that she (Tali) had somehow let down her mother and sister. In the end, after a lengthy struggle, peace settles again in Christy's heart and she starts looking forward to her next life on earth, instead of looking back at the tragedy of the little boy.

The spirits who surround her at Home are supportive of Christy after she staggers away from the bruising death of Laelya. Her regret at leaving Albert and her mother runs deep, and they address her concern for those left behind. They assure her that things will be all right, that she has had a beautiful family, and that she led a "charmed life." As she lies down to rest and tries to think things through fully, benevolent spirits surround her but refrain from seeking to hurry her progress toward her next test.

After Peter has committed suicide, the people Christy knows at Home speak comforting words that make her feel as if she is being hugged, and is safe at last. She is aware of a oneness with them, as if they and she were part of each other's life. Then she gives an explanation for which we may have been waiting:

Do they say anything about the life you just lived?

I was very anxious that I'd done such a bad thing that I would be punished. They said my journey was all the punishment I needed. People are not punished; they punish themselves. I cannot properly have forgiven myself.

Can you now?

Maybe I can. Maybe I can't.

Are they telling you to forgive yourself?

Until I untie myself, it will not come to be. They tell me to be patient and forgive. But they remind me that I can take my time.

But haven't you now forgiven yourself?

I have forgiven myself for the deed. But as long as I act in the same way I'll never let it go.

What is the problem you have to face?

Self-destructive. Greedy. Indulgent. Cowardly. Irresponsible. They tell me I must amend these ways by being patient with myself and not being quick to judge.

(later)

Can you ask for help?

That's a very good idea. They say they do help me, and they are always with me.

(later)

Can you learn your lesson now?
   I will try to.
What is the lesson?
   Love yourself.
And do you?
   I do.

It is the same when Christy reports after Joyce's life, "I have to deal with it myself – like I'm peeling off my skin and starting over." (In view of Hector's self-destruction, this is a remarkable metaphor to use – did her soul silently remember the nature of his death at that moment?)

Peter's return provides an excellent example of the central issue raised in our going Home. Indeed, it may even be the key issue for understanding the whole of this book. Time and time again in cases reported elsewhere, Christy's homeward experience has been cloned. The returning soul is not met with judgment but with a welcome and – above all – with unequivocal acceptance by its spiritual peers. Indeed, we have often been told, even forgiveness is not at issue because to forgive implies judgment, and Home, they say, is not a place of judgment but of totally unconditional love. In response, that same spirit is forced by the power of love to look within itself and to create self-forgiveness and self-love. It is both as amazingly simple and as gigantically challenging as that: as simple, because love is the one and only truly spiritual response to every issue; and as challenging, because once a soul has exercised its freedom to stray from the path of love, it can return only of its own free choice. So loving acceptance becomes the mirror in which the spirit must examine itself. In this way, the apparent weakness of the spirit world's forgiveness in the face of wrongdoing becomes the redemptive strength for the individual soul to choose and create self-forgiveness. It is an overwhelmingly generous and subtle form of non-judgment that is, at the same time, an incredibly effective one.

To understand this idea better we must look at the total picture of the eternal spiritual scene. Souls, Christy included, are sent forth on their journey into the demanding, but exhilarating, environment of planet Earth in order to have selected experiences and from them to learn spiritual lessons. The lessons to be learned may include that list given in Christy's reflection after Peter Boyce's life. Young Peter was self-destructive, greedy, indulgent, cowardly, irresponsible, and above all, unloving toward himself. All this shows quite clearly in the brief snapshot we were given of his life. These are the current lessons for Christy to learn as she returns from Peter's life. But Christy will only truly learn them if she wills it herself. Such is the concept of this training – all of us, without exception, are given (or choose in advance) experiences with lessons attached which we must learn for ourselves. There is no higher authority forcing us to do so; the pathway by which we seek personal maturity is always of our own devising (with a little help from our spiritual friends). No superior power is going to force us to become wise. We must want to be wise. We must find for ourselves the way to true spiritual wisdom.

"So what about mass murderers?" people may ask. "Surely there is retribution?" Of course there is, but it is self-willed and self-administered. There is evidence that those who qualify for the lowest level of Dante's hell – those who, with Satan in Milton's Paradise Lost, proclaim "Evil be thou my good!" – may fall so far outside the thought of self-reclamation that they will need outside spiritual rescue, help, and guidance. It has been reported elsewhere that, eventually, some kind of total reconstitution of the most severely damaged souls will be made by the spirit community. For the rest of us (both author and reader included), the challenge is that we must face squarely those spiritual training issues our present lives bring out, because in life after life, they will return to be faced and dealt with by us, so that eventually we will truly master them. And, we are told, once a lesson has been successfully learned it will not trouble us again.

No doubt someone will ask, "That's all very well, but Christy's life as Sophie, that was most successfully completed, was as some kind of missionary. We don't all have to be *missionaries*, do we?" While it is true that Sophie lived as an unconventional missionary, the heart of her story shows that Christy's real achievement was much broader than that one thing. She overcame the self-indulgence which drove her previously to abandon the lives of both the stillborn child and, especially, the little deaf child. When, as Sophie, she turned up again in the role of a sick child, she fought with determination to get well, and she succeeded. When tempted sexually to "make more money as a whore," as Christy comments, she turned in the other direction. And there was more besides in her life, which all added up to a triumph of self-love. But having such a life still does not let her off the hook. It is said that "One swallow does not make a summer," nor does one successful life complete a heavenly training course. It can get you an A+, but not a degree!

Thinking of Hector and Peter, Christy sees her unsolved problems as those she will have to face time and again. After all, self-forgiveness is a very practical matter. When the trial does come again it must be faced afresh. The consequence of any failure made during our Earth-based spiritual training is to face the issue for as long as it remains one. This is why the spirits took Sophie's cough away. She had succeeded! Physical frailty appears to be a trial she no longer has to endure, at least in that form. Our souls can and do make good progress. Later, Christy faced another kind of frailty in Joyce's life as a bored widow, but she failed that test and had to face the problem by "peeling off all my skin, and starting over."

3. The Return to Earth

After being Hector, Christy returned to earth but we do not have any details. No doubt it took a while before she was ready to return. The next life was as Eleanor. After time at Home the return to a new life came once she could say, "I felt it was time."

Did anyone help you make that decision?
It felt like there was someone there. But they had no form.
Who do you think that might have been?
A helper – it was just a feeling.
Do you think that helper is with you in this life?
Not consciously.
And the helper gave you advice?
It was persuasive. Told me I was ready.
How did you make the next arrangement?
It suddenly was. The light grows dimmer. Being born: I felt drawn. I knew it was time. I was a little boy, Franklyn.

Christy feels in this passage that she had some help in making her decision, and hints that the spiritual help came from one who may be present in her new life as well. (Belief that we have spirit guides is quite well-established.) Some souls have reported a process of viewing their new parents in advance of making a decision, indeed of having a limited choice of families after stating their preferences. This pre-viewing of a life-situation was not found in Christy's reports though there is an indication that some choice was made.

Sophie's life also starts with a decision-making process. After the life as the stillborn, the shaken Christy is told that she must try again; she cannot stay at Home forever. She is anxious about the process. She made the decision which parents to use for the previous life but it did not work out well. "They make suggestions, describe people to me." There is still a choice of parents for her to make.

Then she adds an interesting comment: "I think there are other people there – the usual bunch. Some leave when they have to." One well-established idea is that souls work in a loose-knit team with other souls, with whom they frequently reincarnate as a group. This may be why, several times, Christy identified people in a past life with those she knows in her present existence. After

Laeyla, for example, she identified her mother in that life with her current close friend Rebecca, and her former husband as another friend, Ewan. The relationships are not the same, nor are they intended to be. Even our most beloved partners do not necessarily re-appear in the same role, but may be a distant cousin or our high school teacher. After being the deaf baby, Christy declares, "I've decided I'm going to be a fighter." She chooses her parents and then is born. To her evident relief she notes that although she is small, she is "OK." True to her word, she makes a success of her life as Sophie.

Finally, the birth process seems to have a two-way pull. Not only is Christy, post-Tali, making herself ready to return to Earth, but she declares the process as actually pulling her toward her new mother: "Magnetic – I'm drawn to this woman."

4. Living at Home

Neither during her commentary in hypnosis, nor in our conversations afterwards, did Christy ever express any doubts about the existence of Home. She moved to and from her various lives, from Earth to Home and back again, with confidence and no sense of surprise. She did not consciously bring any special theological viewpoint with her to the sessions, only the secular, slightly cynical curiosity about matters spiritual which is typical of the young European, not least the British. Nor, frankly, did she give me the feeling that this celestial aspect of her journey was an exotic or awe-inspiring experience for her; it was far too natural and far too pleasant. I am sure that Christy believes in the existence of Home, now that she has had time in which to process this information, and is relaxed about it. She no more doubts the experience of Home than she doubts the reality of her past lives. Having watched her emotions as she went through the process of traveling to and from Home, I do not have any doubts about them either. It's where we all belong.

14
Christy's Life Patterns

5 Female lives (average age 58 years)
7 Male lives (average age 12 years)

Name	Sex	Age at Death	Cause of Death	Country
Hector	M	30	Suicide	Italy
Eleanor	F	73	Natural death	Scotland
Franklyn	M	7	Bubonic plague	France
Saera	F	60	Natural death	England
Silvio	M	18	Stabbed in a fight	Italy
The Stillborn	M	Fetus	Died in womb	unknown
Deaf Baby	M	4/12	Cot death	unknown
Sophie	F	60	Natural death	Corsica
Tali	M	10	Murdered	Mali
Laeyla	F	45	Abnormal pregnancy	England
Peter	M	18	Suicide	England
Joyce	F	50	Accident	United States

Christy reported twelve lives, five female and seven male. There was a marked difference between her experience of the two sexes. For a start the women lived on average nearly fifty-eight years, three of them dying of natural causes, the other two accidentally. Those dying in old age typified a normal lifespan for their time. The men and boys were quite different. Their average age at death was less than twelve years, and they all died unnaturally: Hector and Peter committed suicide, Silvio died in a fight, Tali was murdered, and Franklyn died of disease. We do not know the medical reason why the little Fetus and the Deaf Baby gave up their lives, but Christy probably abandoned both of them in a panic.

Overall this appears quite a grim picture. It is not surprising that Christy seemed to identify most strongly with female lives, accepting that her really difficult lives were male:

> *It is always boys, the boys have trouble.*

Do you become a boy for a reason?

> *Trials – it makes me a stronger woman. The things I do as a woman, I can do because of the trials. I feel it's a balance, a payoff. I'm sad for the boys – they have troubles – but I seem to benefit from it: I have courage.*

What qualities do the spirits want you to work on?

> *They know I have a tendency to be angry, pre-occupied. They want me to try and see things, have perspective.*

Personality

The life patterns I look for when viewing a number of past lives are those that have relevance for my client's present life. In a sense the detail of how we lived in the past is less relevant than the aspects of our personality we carry forward from life to life.

Distressing as it is to believe that Christy may have been involved in a crime of passion when she was in Hector's body, this is not the long-term judgment we should make. We took no lengthy recording of her return Home on that sad occasion, only just enough to learn of her feeling forgiven, but after other lives she grappled with similar spiritual issues. Tali's return Home evoked the remarks cited above, and we may see their application. The anger that boiled in Tali's breast after he and the members of his family and village were assassinated had a precursor in Hector's wild anger at discovering his wife's adultery. Silvio was a hurt and angry boy whose relations with his father were painful, but not as painful as the seething anger expressed by Peter several times toward his violent and disloyal father. One may wonder whether anger at becoming pregnant again could have been the underlying *energetic* cause of Laeyla's tragic end. Christy also struggled against the threefold challenge of physical weakness in the lives of the Stillborn, the Deaf Baby (where she certainly brought that life to an early end by angrily abandoning him), and then in Sophie's frailty. Sophie's triumph over weakness, anger, and frustration was rewarded by the gift of the handsome Louis, by her supportive traveling companion, Felix the horse, and by the spirits' eventual removal of her hallmark persistent cough.

If anger appears as a recurrent theme of a negative kind, so independence of spirit was clearly a positive indicator of Christy's enduring strength. We pass with Hector, but independence is seen to be operating at full blast as Eleanor takes to the road as a minstrel in search of a better life. She knows what is good for her, however. Music takes her only as far as John's Perthshire farmhouse, where she trades her rugged individuality for settled domestic bliss.

Independence is so strongly developed a trait of Christy today that it is hardly surprising to see this characteristic cropping up many times. Saera, who is branded as "willful" by members of the Order, wanders off to Ireland in search of selfhood. Silvio robs a baker for food as a boy, and as he turns the corner into manhood he fights with his peers for sport. Sophie's itinerant evangelism for many years, over countless miles of dusty French roads, is the very epitome of independence. As for Peter, while his angry rebellion against society is sad, it is at the same time a sign of his severely wounded spirit bravely struggling to assert its own independence.

Even in the lame, bored life of Joyce we see faint traces of this quality coming through. She may have been crushed by society's attitudes toward black people, including her parents' compliance with the prevailing norms of the white community, but still she struggled to do the right thing. She hired Joshua, though her parents would never have dreamed of employing a black gardener. She rightly saw that the issue with the scalding water was not related to her admiration for Joseph's rugged physique, but to her breach of the social norm. Married, she stuck it out grimly with her dreadful drunken husband, and wisely discounted the feeling that she should have pretended grief at his death, when truly she felt none. On the surface, and in its ending, Joyce's life appears lame, but she was a fighter underneath.

Other Characteristics

Personality issues are not the only themes we may choose to note. Sexuality is a very obvious one. Hector's infatuation with his beloved wife, the model for the statue of Epiphany, leads him to take her life in a frenzy of uncontrollable rage. Centuries later, Eleanor is calmer. Her love for Bob is physically short-lived but intense, and passion for her lost lover endures throughout her successful and sexually fulfilled marriage to John. Saera seems to be without much interest in sex. Her inner struggle with the shadows may have given her enough to grapple with during her life, and she was, by her own account, somewhat masculine in appearance and outlook. The glimpse we have of Silvio's sexuality is crude and fleeting, but when we come to Sophie it is entirely another story.

Sophie fell in love with Louis, her staunch childhood companion. He it was who had lent the sick girl his horse, and he fell in love with this fragile but determined person as she drove herself from sickness into health. Without doubt, her improved health was partly due to fresh air and exercise, but mostly due to the gift that Louis brought, as their mutual love refreshed and renewed her whole self. Whether her passion for him, like Hector's for his wife, was just too immense, or whether Louis simply had another agenda, we cannot tell, but his ambition took him away to Paris and threw her into deep despair at his going. Just as Eleanor had never given up in her remembrance of Bob the lute player, so Sophie never gave up thinking about and praying for Louis. He was to be her only physical lover (of that Christy was certain). Whether she turned down opportunities to settle down at one of the farms she visited, as Eleanor had settled down with John, we cannot say, but she died full of love for Louis, and was sure that by remaining true she had done the right thing in his memory, difficult though it may have been.

Laeyla's story is so different. Here the marriage to her husband was an untroubled love affair until she became pregnant for the second time in her forties. Observing Christy's recollection of the couple's wedding night was a riot! She giggled and smirked in hypnotic trance, and told me quite firmly that we had to come back later. Her subsequent avowal that she had been the far side of the bedroom door cuts no ice with me! Certainly their happy marriage was successful in material terms as the apothecary business grew and prospered. She had a beautiful daughter and high hopes – until her second pregnancy. What exactly happened to poor Laeyla remained unexplained by Christy, but her death spelled the abrupt end of her most fulfilling marriage.

In contrast, Peter's adolescent desires to attract girls seem rather forlorn, but girls were certainly on his mind when he developed the appalling rash that drove his alcohol-deranged mind over the top. "No girl in her right mind would look at me now," one of his last drunken thoughts before committing suicide, suggests that he expected to bear the pockmarks of the rash on his face for the rest of his life. Peter may have been rough, but he was aware of his sexuality, and he cared about losing his wild and attractively curly hair when it fell to the ground under the army barber's scissors.

Joyce enjoyed her wedding in a sadly conformist way. She felt very pretty in her beautiful dress. She was happy that her father looked proud of her, even though her husband was twenty-two years her senior and – like so many young brides – she knew that she really did not love him. But though tormented by the race issue and by her disastrous marriage, Joyce retained a level head when it came to the homosexuality of her younger brother, Jeff. She tried to like his male friends and refused to stand in judgment over them. She left her wealth to Jeff in her will, out of sibling affection. She was a shy, hesitant woman who struggled to make sense of it all, doing a rather better job of coping with stress than her self-criticism and the final, unhappy, alcohol-related accident suggest.

Music is Christy's current passion. Hector was artistic, a sculptor. Eleanor, Sophie, and Laeyla were needlewomen. Sophie enjoyed hearing the pipes, but only Eleanor was known to be a true musician. Her gift of improvisation is one which Christy shares today. Christy had other characteristics worth noting. As Eleanor, she was feminine with long, dark, straight hair; Saera was probably androgynous in her youth, with black hair and an appearance she described as "thin, hard, pale, strong." Peter Boyce, in addition to having an incipient beard and hairs on his chest, was "pretty tall, with blue eyes and unruly, curly brown hair." Tali's skin color was black and he probably had dark curly hair to match. The point of such physical investigation is that it allows us to assert that the human locus for our ongoing spiritual life has no connection with any one family, class, race, color, or continent. Other studies have shown a wider net being flung by individual spirits – the recurrence of the British Isles in Christy's story is not really typical. I had expected at least one life to have been lived in east or central Europe, India, or Asia, for example. However, we only recorded twelve lives. Had we attempted more there would be a greater variety of locations and types of people.

However much we try to analyze the story of Christy's past lives, the real issue for her today is whether she can see in her present life echoes of the past that she would like to develop further, or might wish to avoid and suppress. The musical theme, with which we started her fascinating story, remains a happy and productive one. Christy is a talented musician who is looking in the future to develop a musical career. Let us wish her well as she takes the resonance of Eleanor's playing before King Edward I of England, and draws upon its ancient harmonics in the days to come. Let us hope also that she will always maintain the strength and rugged individuality of her past, and enjoy a long, happy, and fulfilling life this time around.

15
Reincarnation

What sense can we make for ourselves of Christy's journey through twelve past lives?

Now that we have shown that someone in hypnosis can discover all kinds of disaster and mayhem in their history, I imagine many readers may feel rather wary of venturing down the uncharted track of their past lives. Christy did not consciously know anything of the experiences she was going to have in trance. But, having been duly warned, she braved the possibilities and found out the hard way. In one sense, the spiritual Christy already knew the whole of her story. It seems likely that we all must remember something of our past, if only from our dream life. But as the mists of past lives fade in our babyhood, most of us have almost total amnesia and our past is increasingly hidden; even our recurring dreams and nightmares are not easily believed.

Research has shown that one in five hundred children possesses the ability to remember something of his most recent past life – and even on occasion to speak a foreign language he has known before (*xenoglossy* is the technical term). These abilities are usually quickly suppressed under the disbelieving gaze of the adult world, which does not take kindly to the idea of rebirth over a long series of lives. Most religious training and our natural human skepticism make it hard for us to believe in things we do not ordinarily and readily experience. So it seems appropriate to examine briefly the idea of reincarnation (having a succession of human lives) before taking leave of Christy's engaging testimony.

Is this book really about memories of past lives, or is it a fairy-tale fiction? You will be willingly forgiven if you opt for the fairy-tale approach, but you should know about the large quantity of literature with accounts of similar life histories, presented by psychiatrists, psychologists, and clinical hypnotists for their professional colleagues to examine. Frankly, there is nothing unusual in Christy's tale except, perhaps, the high degree of trouble it tells. This may even be seen as a testimony to its truthfulness. The simple teller of fairy stories likes to show us good winning over evil, ease winning over difficulty, and success winning over failure, but the story of Christy's past is much more believable because it shows her soul's genuine but unfinished struggle to understand the way of spiritual integrity. I believe there is all the more reason to see it as true because it is so roughhewn. Christy's present life, it is good to note, appears to continue the success themes from the lives of Eleanor, Saera, Sophie, and Laeyla.

When people talk about reincarnation they often raise issues of their belief and religious doctrine. Because of ingrained teachings, such people appear sometimes unwilling to consider that religion can be based on genuine experience, rather than on theological theories. We may declare whether we believe or disbelieve in reincarnation, but when facts appear (even of the type Christy provides) suggesting a definite answer, we must be able to discard our purely theoretical point of view – right or wrong – and make an honest evaluation of which facts are relevant, and what conclusions we should draw from them.

Christy herself is quite secular; as a modern young British woman she has little time for organized religion and is largely unacquainted with it. The hypnosis sessions I gave her invoked no magic, no sense of an awesome and fascinating mystery, which would cause her to have a sudden spiritual awakening. Nor was Christy ever subjected to demonic powers of any kind, despite the fears of those who doubt the spiritual integrity of hypnotherapy.

My background is in Christian parish ministry, and as a clinical hypnotist I often use regression techniques in my work, usually taking clients back in thought to their childhood. The sessions with Christy were totally unprepared, routine in nature, and perfectly relaxed. The only thing different about them was that we decided to explore several past lives, if they were available to her, and record whatever might turn up. And, with astonishing ease and clarity, we turned up rebirth after rebirth, plus happy and fulfilling experiences in between her past lives – nothing out of the ordinary and certainly nothing of which to be frightened or "disbelieving."

Perhaps Christy's story does not speak strongly enough for you to decide upon the matter – that's fair. But the issue is not one of believing or disbelieving in one individual's account. Have you heard the amusing old Indian question: "How many elephants do the British need to see before they can believe there is such an animal?" Whatever your reaction to Christy, it is well to remember that there are now in existence records of *millions* of people before her who have experienced past lives in therapeutic sessions. Millions of people after her will do so as well, as more and more therapists see the value of past-life regression, and more and more clients respond enthusiastically to the literature published on the subject.

In her book *Past-life Therapy, the State of the Art* (1995), Dr. Rabia Lynn Clark reported a survey she made of 256 members of the Association of Past-Life Research and Therapies, each having a minimum of five years in the work of past-life regression. On the question of reincarnation, a whopping 93% of the practitioners said they believed in it, and the rest were neutral; not one dissented. An even larger 99% believed past lives affect present lives. This implied that the professionals most engaged in this kind of work appear remarkably sure that reincarnation is an idea of merit and substance.

How can we account for the negative attitude held by some who were probably brought up in an organized religious belief system? Religions are founded on ancient ideas of what the world is like, why and how it started, and what is going to happen to it in the end. There have been many extraordinary myths of ancient history, including one that a big turtle plods across the sky carrying the sun on its back. Another told of the bright sun being drawn across the heavens by prancing horses, pulling it in a great chariot. The biblical model of the universe, known to Jews and Christians alike, contains references to "waters above the firmament" (the sky) and "waters below the firmament" (the sea). The star-studded heaven was envisioned as being arched above the Earth. The Earth was flat and thick and circular, with Sheol, the place of the dead, contained deep in its middle. It stood on great pillars in the water which lay under and around the Earth. It was pictured (to use a modern description) rather like a gigantic pizza on a stand, with a blue mixing bowl over the top, all of it being totally submerged in a fish tank filled with water!

Images like these had value in explaining the unknown to earlier generations. They were inspired guesses, not scientific discoveries, although people at the time may have taken them literally. Despite the notion of absolute truth that some adherents grant to the words of the Jewish, Christian, and Islamic scriptures, only a few adherents to any of these faiths believe today in the cosmic model of the universe laid out in the Bible that I have just recalled.

When Nicolaus Copernicus published *The Little Commentary* around 1514, he was putting into shape observations that had been in gestation throughout the mathematical community of his day. Indeed his major work on the physical nature of the universe might never have been published had it not been for the support of Georg Joachim Rheticus, a young professor of mathematics and astronomy at the University of Wittenberg. Their efforts led, a century later, to the astronomical discoveries of Galileo Galilei, whose telescopes, and physical observations of the solar system published in 1632, brought up to date work that Copernicus had done. Galileo then incurred the wrath of the Church, which banned the distribution of his books.

Go forward just another fifty-five years to 1687, to the publication in England by Sir Isaac Newton of his great *Principia*, explaining the law of universal gravitation. His book took the work done by Copernicus and Galileo a stage further. One discovery led to another and that one to another, as it so often does in the sciences. We can go on to describe Albert Einstein's *General Theory of Relativity*, which greatly expanded Newton's physics.

Hypnotists, psychiatrists, and others professionally engaged in past-life regression belong to the great tradition of scientific inquiry. They are not engaged in creating an alternative religious system, but are simply expressing the truth of our experiences. In the same way that Copernicus, Galileo, Newton, and Einstein touched on the nature of life and were bound to interact with theology, so do we. Over the centuries society has given to religion the task of explaining the nature of the human and the divine. In explaining our findings from clients' past-life regression sessions, we will inevitably raise religious questions and even excite religious intolerance. But that's in the nature of things, and it is right that we should do so. Religion has a vital role to play in the life of the human community. It is there to explore what is speculative and what is known, what is dangerous and what is good, and to turn its findings into theological statements. Theology follows discoveries and revelations; it never leads – and probably never should initiate change!

When the Christian church reacted against the new view of the universe put forward by Copernicus and Galileo it was, historically speaking, only attempting to do its job of testing the soundness and correctness of their revised world view. Today there is little doubt that religion is overwhelmingly attuned to the Copernican world view. Religion is not always fighting a rearguard action against science, as has oftentimes been imagined, but religion is cautious because it performs the very necessary task of safeguarding and interpreting the truth, standards, and morals of society.

As we engage in past-life regression, therapists may not see themselves as scientists, but discovery of the human phenomenon of rebirth should be seen for what it is. It is a discovery about the facts of our being human. It is a discovery that makes even more sense now that Einstein has shown how energy creates the material world. Reincarnation is a fact, the discovery of which may eventually require the Catholic church to reconsider its idea of purgatory, Hinduism to refashion its idea of karma, and so on. We have found ourselves involved in uncovering this truth, finding out about the way the universal spiritual forces operate in our lives. It is a discovery that will prove of monumental help in taming the violent, self-centered world of which we are a part.

This book is not the place for detailed examination of the Bible, the Upanishads, the Tibetan Book of the Dead, or other scriptural writings concerning the idea of reincarnation. The question is whether this idea – which is as ancient as history itself – is only a theory after all. If religious thinking has been willing to absorb the world view of Copernicus and Galileo, Newton's gravity, and Einstein's quantum physics, is there any reason why evidence of reincarnation, believed now by a large number of well-qualified medical and scientific practitioners, should not receive the same level of acceptance? I leave that issue for your consideration; I have made up my mind, and, as you may have guessed, my conversion to the idea of reincarnation is a direct result of witnessing past-life regressions first hand, and of finding strong evidence that others, better qualified than I, have done the same.

If the "rebirth" of our spirits in a series of bodies is a fact, what are its implications? The current belief is that your spirit and mine are involved in a long and complex spiritual training course. It causes us to inhabit the body of a child, then to live out that person's life, however long or short it may be, facing its challenges, learning its spiritual lessons, and then returning Home for rest, refreshment, renewal, and further preparation. It is a cycle that is repeated and repeated as we progress (or fail to make progress) toward our goal of complete spiritual maturity.

Let me deal briefly with the idea of spiritual maturity, because its implications are important. While thoughtful individuals have said that people have souls, very little of our human activity is openly based upon that spiritual concept. For example, we largely ignore the practical issue of what actually happens to a baby's indwelling spirit when it takes the plunge and enters into the child. Is the way we should welcome this tender spirit into our family *before birth* fully understood? Remember Christy's stillborn baby? The father was shouting at the mother that the child she was bearing was not his offspring. There was also possibly physical violence in that situation. In any case, Christy, already within the fetus, felt his little body grow cold, and so she left it. Do we really understand how babies are affected by our attitude while they are still in the womb? What kind of welcome do we prepare for our children's spirits?

Then comes the issue of the Deaf Baby, illustrated by Christy's cot death experience. Here the parents were loving and welcoming to the child, but the struggle for Christy to overcome the handicaps of the child's feeble body proved just too much for her. It is clear that the parents were not to blame, and that Christy may have given up the struggle too soon, but the concept is instructive. When we take a child into our home, we take a gentle, possibly very fragile spirit along with the baby whose body we see and nurture. As we dump our baby off with a child-minder, are we always adequately aware of that? As we adults shout at one another, do we ever consider the feeling of despair we may create in our baby's soul?

Three times Christy's story points to major difficulties with fathers. The angry father of the Stillborn was one. Another was the father who meted out rough treatment to Silvio, the Italian urchin who was rarely called by his proper name, and who grew up to fend for himself because his father did not truly care about his welfare. In consequence, without sufficient nurture, Silvio became a roughneck, expressing his anger at life by stealing and fighting. The third father's violence and disloyalty to his family left Peter horribly scarred for life, and also bore some responsibility for Peter's own dishonesty, violence, and final self-negation. If Peter's father could not love him, why should he try to love himself?

The consequences in three other cases are more speculative. Eleanor did not know her father and developed a sturdy, almost masculine independence. The unknown parentage of Saera is puzzling: was she possessed by her "shadows" perhaps because she couldn't be certain who her parents might be? Did Joyce's lackluster life reflect the manipulative approach of her father (and possibly her mother), who thought it fit for a shy young woman of twenty to marry a rich, belligerent drunk more than twice her age? Lastly, we have a removal of fatherly protection in Tali's grim tale. Here the father appears to have acted for the good of his family and village by going off in search of more fruitful land, but he failed to return because healso had been slaughtered by enemies.

There are also parental successes. Eleanor's mother, apparently without her partner, brings up a musical and self-assured daughter, well groomed and prepared to play her harp before the King. Most obviously, Sophie, though sickly in her body, received loving support as a child from her parents. When the time came for her to take off on her own as a missionary, they seem to have let her go in the pious hope that all would be well, as she was consumed with thankfulness to God for saving her when she fell off her horse. As we nurture and care for our growing children, we need to remember that they and we are in a close, intimate team of souls who return time and time again together, but in a variety of different relationships and for many different life purposes.

Though Christy was disappointed in love during some of her lives, only Joyce's marital experience seems to have been truly awful. But there is much to be said about our relationships, whether expressed in terms of deep affection or more basically in sexual acts. In all such activity our souls are living out issues of self-worth for all concerned. Sex is not meant to be the power one party exercises over another, but the sharing of delight between two lives, both physical and spiritual. In this precious human activity lies the opportunity for us to be true to our spiritual calling, even if it means remaining true only to our vision of the perfect relationship. That was the case for Eleanor, who, long after she had married farmer John, fondly remembered Bob the musician, and for Sophie, who remembered her lover Louis during her remaining life of single blessedness.

Some of the issues of being souls-in-training relate to aspects of life that do not feature strongly in Christy's account. Work is a good example. Eleanor is seen mending clothes as well as playing her harp; she fights off intruders at the farm, raises two children, helps her husband in the fields. Sacra takes charge in the Order and is heavily occupied in its activities of teaching and healing. Sophie sews, evangelizes, delivers babies, teaches children, helps with families. Laeyla makes cloth, supports her mother's activities, raises her daughter, and keeps a good home for her beloved husband. These are the women. The boys mostly die too young to make much of a mark, though Hector appears to be successful as a sculptor. (I don't believe this particular client's experience represents a fair comparison of the two genders' overall performance.) Christy, who as a soul is without gender, indicated that she knowingly undertook major challenges when she chose male lives. She certainly was tested! So work is one means by which we may progress spiritually on our journey.

Spirituality and religious belief have only two expressions in this book: in a vague sort of way during Saera's life, and very definitely during Sophie's life. Clearly it was spiritually positive that Sophie was thankful to God for saving her when she fell. One gets the feeling, however, that belief and piety play a relatively minor role. The practical, everyday, mundane issues of life comprise the principal medium of spiritual expression, and include such emotional contrasts as hatred and love, anger and forgiveness, greed and honesty – all the things that make up the totality of our personality, good and bad.

So when, life after life, Christy returns, exhausted or exhilarated, from her latest trip to Earth, she relaxes and thinks by herself in the whispering, warm, comforting, familiar environment of Home, about all the things she did and said. The spiritual guides and her spirit-friends praise and forgive her, and help her to re-adjust her thinking as she prepares for another try. So the time comes for rebirth into a physical body – re-incarnation. It is as simple and as natural as that. It is a process that seers, mystics, visionaries, psychics, and people of wise understanding have spoken about for thousands of years, and it is just as true now as it ever was. For Christy today, reincarnation is not a dry academic issue to be debated seriously and turned into wordy theological propositions. It is just part of the natural rhythm of her life. Nor is reincarnation a religious proposition to be used for its persuasive power. It is simply a fact relating to the wholeness of an eternal life that stretches far beyond the conscious mind's comprehension, but not beyond the realm of the subconscious mind.

Conclusion

During this, our latest reincarnation, Christy's soul and mine chose to meet or were guided to meet, so that we might be able to make a book of these truths to enrich your thinking. Now your beautiful soul may grapple with what we have learned together and make whatever you can of it all. It is not a light matter either to believe or disbelieve in reincarnation, because the outcome may change the whole way you look at life and the way you live your life from now on. It has for many people, including Christy and me.

May love guide your thoughts and your path always.

Other O-books of interest

Angels In Our Time

Why they're here, where to see them and how to work with them

ISHVARA D'ANGELO

CONTENT: In 1990 Ishvara D'Angelo was a leading figure in aromatherapy and a practising Buddhist when she had a powerful experience of an angel. She changed the direction of her life, her name (from Patricia Davis), left aromatherapy, and began painting angels.

This book goes far beyond the fuzzy feel-good messages in many others. You will find suggestions about meditation, visualisation and prayer, ways of communicating with Angels and identifying your personal Guardian. But you will also find ideas about the way the Angels ask you conduct your life from day to day, ranging from conflict resolution, relationships and healing to your choice of career and practical suggestions about how to go about that. Topics such as the food we eat, the clothes we wear, the cars we drive, which bank we choose to trust with our savings are all part of the life of Spirit that the Angels ask us to live.

Above all, we are called to help combat the forces of greed and ignorance that threaten the whole Planet. The Archangels are calling on us to make decisions, sometimes difficult ones, and take an active part in that struggle. But we never stand alone: they are always with us and ready to guide us – so long as we will listen.

Author: Ishvara d'Angelo is the author of *An A-Z of Aromatherapy*, which has sold over a quarter of a million copies worldwide, and several other bestselling titles. She now lives in Totnes, England.

Reviews and endorsements:

Angels in our Time *lives up to its title and brings a lively and fresh approach to working with the angelic kingdom. Even though Ishvara explains some traditional ideas about angels, her main concern is to help her readers to open their own 21st century hearts to the angels, encouraging us to meet the angels now, in our own way, not relying on old fashioned theologies. In the tradition of William Blake, Ishvara sees angels and then tells everyone who will listen! She includes some very beautiful meditations to help the reader open to the different angel families, and to the four Archangels, as well as stories from people she meets in her workshops. What a delight that the angels have guided her to O books who have been able to include her wonderful pictures in full colour.*

Ishvara's book will have to be on every angel lover's shelf. Ishvara is a genuine visionary who has been working with angels for since 1990, when she had a wonderful vision of her own. Since then she has been creating beautiful paintings that do not rely on the Christmas card images, but are inspired by her real, intimate experiences. Ishvara's words and pictures will shift your consciousness and you are quite likely to wake in the night to see an angel seated on your bed! **Theolyn Cortens,** author of *Living with Angels* and *Working with Your Guardian Angels*

[1 905047 87 8   £11.99]

The Art of Being Psychic

The power to free the artist within

JUNE-ELLENI LAINE

CONTENT: Psychic ability still remains a bit of a mystery to most, and yet we all have the potential to tap into the under-utilized areas of the brain in order to gain access to a world of creativity. Contacting the "creative source" and thinking outside the box of our own limitations in the style of artists as diverse as Da Vinci and Mozart up to Einstein and George Lucas of today, doesn't come easily. However, with the right tools, and a clear sense of purpose, we can develop our ability, learning to enter altered states at will, to produce art that exceeds our normal expectations.

This book shares the enjoyment of psychic art and removes the "Myst" from "Mystic", leaving the "I.C." moments. It offers a new perspective on self-awareness that has the power to liberate the artist within us all. Balancing intuition and logic, right and left-brain thinking, mind, body and spirit, will inevitably strengthen our connection to a source capable of producing much more than anything we already know.

AUTHOR: *June-Elleni Laine* is one of the worlds leading psychic artists and teachers in this field, appearing on TV and running a schedule of workshops, demonstrations and lectures. Visit **www.psychicartworks.com**

As a companion to the book, a Audio CD has been produced adding the powerful dimension of sound! This audio companion is ideal for those who intend to develop their psychic ability. It features multi-dimensional sounds specifically created to resonate with subtle frequencies of the mind, body and soul. For more information or to order a copy of the CD click on www.psychicartworks.com

Endorsements & Reviews:

A brilliant book for anyone wishing to develop their intuition, creativity and psychic ability. It is truly wonderful, one of the best books on psychic development that I have read. Fascinating and thought provoking exercises abound and open one up to an awareness of the right/left brain functions and how to balance them. Readers are shown how to access their creative right brain and so tap into their intuitive knowledge and psychic ability, this in turn opens the door to spirit communication. **Suzanna McInerney** – former President, College of Psychic Studies, London

[1 905047 54 1]   £12.99

Beyond Photography

Encounters with orbs, angels and mysterious light forms!

KATIE HALL AND JOHN PICKERING

CONTENT: John and Katie used to be sceptical (to put it mildly) about crop circles, angels, ghosts, fairies, UFOs and all other aspects of the paranormal.

But a few years ago, as they photographed the grounds of their new house, they started to find the most extraordinary images appearing on their prints. Though professional designers and photographers, they couldn't explain them.

They soon realised that their experience was not unique. Orbs have been appearing all over the world over the last few years. First dismissive, then intrigued, this is the fullest personal account in the world of one couple's experience of this new phenomenon. Documented by thousands of incredible photographs, their journey has led them inexorably to some extraordinary conclusions. There are realities running parallel to ours. We are not the dominant life form on this planet. We share this world with a super non-human intelligence which interacts with human consciousness.
It is an intelligence that is empathic, symbiotic and multifaceted; they call it 'LIGHT-FORMS!' – and, if they are correct, it is right next to you, right now!

Authors: John Pickering and Katie Hall are professional designers and illustrators. They live in England.

Endorsements and reviews:

I have known John for many years now and been with him on many orb photo shoots. I can testify that these incredible images are genuine and authentically captured. Whether this is new phenomena or something that has always been with us and which we are now able to see via the digital technology, I cannot say, but through my own experience, which is confirmed by the work of John and Katie, I do know there seems to be a consciousness present with these orbs which appears to react and interact with us. The powerful images in this book will, I am sure, help us to open our minds to other realities and other possibilities. **Mike Oram** Award-winning landscape photographer

The authors invite you to join them on a fascinating quest; a voyage of discovery into the nature of a phenomenon, manifestations of which are shown as being historical and global as well as contemporary and intently personal.

En route they check their own extraordinary encounters against the findings, thoughts and beliefs of scientists, writers, philosophers and spiritual thinkers along with the everyday testimonies of other curious and questioning individuals across several centuries.

Brian Sibley *Writer and Broadcaster.*

[9781905047901] £12.99

O books
O is a symbol of the world, of oneness and unity. In different cultures it also means the "eye", symbolizing knowledge and insight, and in Old English it means "place of love or home". O books explores the many paths of understanding which different traditions have developed down the ages, particularly those today that express respect for the planet and all of life. In philosophy, metaphysics and aesthetics O as zero relates to infinity, indivisibility and fate. In Zero Books we are developing a list of provocative shorter titles that cross different specializations and challenge conventional academic or majority opinion.

For more information on the full list of over 300 titles please visit our website
www.O-books.net

BOOKS